CW00385879

**British Library Cataloguing in Publication
Data**
　Protz, Roger
　European beer almanac.
　1. Beers　2. Europe
　I. Title
　641.23094

　ISBN 0-948403-28-4

Typeset in 9½ on 9½pt Century Old Style by
Chapterhouse,
Formby L37 3PX

Printed in Scotland
by Eagle Colourbooks

Publisher's Note
All information given in the following pages was
correct at the time of printing.

Come, my master, Ill bring you to
the best beer in Europe
– *Christopher Marlowe*, Dr Faustus, 1588

C O N T E N T S

ACKNOWLEDGEMENTS

I am grateful to the brewers, shippers, wholesalers, retailers, trade associations, embassies and trade missions who have responded to my letters, phone calls and faxes with a flood of information about the beers they brew or distribute.

A few words of special thanks go to Michael Cook of Continental Lager Distributors of Croydon, Surrey, who helped with information from the USSR (where companies only respond to letters written in Russian); to Richard Larkin and Iain Loe of the Campaign for Real Ale, seasoned travellers in Europe and a fund of useful knowledge´ and to fellow beer writer, Michael Jackson, who opened a few doors that would otherwise have stayed firmly shut. Michaels pioneering books, *The New World Guide to Beer* (Bloomsbury) and the *Pocket Beer Book* (Mitchell Beazley), are written with enormous enthusiasm and researched with awesome diligence; they should be on every beer lovers bookshelf. Finally my special thanks to my wife, Diana, and her colleagues in the modern languages department of South Thames College, Putney, London, who translated my letters into the relevant European languages.

INTRODUCTION

Beer is back on the agenda. The convulsions in
Europe, the falling of walls and barriers, the ending
of old antagonisms and a new spirit of unity and
common endeavour have brought with them an
appreciation of the worlds oldest alcoholic drink.
Beer was first brewed in Ancient Egypt and
Mesopotamia but Europe is the cradle both of
modern brewing and of styles that predate the arrival
of the hop plant and new technologies that
encouraged the development of lagering.

For most of my lifetime, beer was something that
people drank without much thought or appreciation.
It was a pleasant brown liquid that encouraged
conviviality but did not inspire flights of thought or
great research. Drinkers would prefer one brand to
another because it tasted better. Few thought to ask
why. 'Respectable' people drank wine, not beer, at
home and became quite knowledgeable on the
subject. They could tell claret from Burgundy and
could describe in some detail the advantages of using
Pinot Noir or Cabernet Sauvignon grapes. But if you
had suggested that Maris Otter was a finer malting
barley than Pipkin or that Goldings had a better hop
aroma than Fuggles, they would have dismissed you
as a crank.

Such attitudes are changing fast. A large
supermarket near my home, twenty miles north of
London, has a section devoted to European beer,
including wheat beers from Germany and ales
produced by the Trappist monks of Chimay in
Belgium. Such a choice would have been unthinkable

two or three years ago. But suddenly people are aware that beer is more than a pint of bitter or a can of international lager. In Britain, the Campaign for Real Ale has challenged the hegemony of the giant brewers and, almost single-handed, has created a climate in which choice and a flood of independent and micro-brewers can flourish. In Belgium and the Netherlands, consumer groups PINT and the *Objectieve Bierproevers* carry out similar work. In Germany and Czechoslovakia, beer drinkers political parties have been formed to contest elections in defence of quality and tradition. Newspapers and magazines now welcome beer writers. Radio and television programmes discuss beer.

Drinkers are now aware of the abundant choice throughout Europe which is available within easy reach. The simple division between the ales of Britain and the lagers of the rest of Europe will no longer suffice. Ales are brewed in mainland Europe, too. Belgium, in particular, has a style of top-fermenting beers that is as honourable and ancient as the British method and certainly more idiosyncratic owing to the use of fruit as well as malt and a fermentation process that encourages wild yeasts to turn sweet wort into alcohol. Ales are also brewed in Germany, thought of as the epitome of an all-lager culture. Germany has wheat beers and '*Altbiers*' – old beers – and even some of its lagers are as dark as a British mild.

Perhaps the greatest revelation to British drinkers is that lager is not a term of abuse! Lager beers from the mainland have taste, character and great complexity and can stand comparison with the finest cask-conditioned ales. If this book achieves nothing else I hope it will restore the term Pilsener to its rightful place in the pantheon of brewing.

The book is *not* called the Best Beers of Europe. That would be a quite different book, one that would require you to spend years on the hoof. I am offering a selection of beer and a snapshot of the quality and choice available. Few people will have the time enjoyed by a professional beer writer to visit the leading brewing regions. The lynchpin of the book is that all the beers included are available outside the country of origin so that you will have comparatively easy access to them. Some famous brands such as

Heineken and Stella Artois are not included because they are brewed under licence in other countries. This can cause confusion for consumers; the regular Heineken brewed in Britain by Whitbread, for example, is some 12° of gravity less than the regular Dutch version, now sold in Britain as Heineken Export.

How beer is brewed

It is widely understood now that a major difference between ales and lager beers is that one uses a top-fermenting yeast and the other a bottom-fermenting variety. But that difference can be exaggerated. Yeast is a single cell micro-organism that feeds on sweet liquids and in the process produces alcohol and carbon dioxide. It is highly adaptable and will change its characteristics if it is moved from one fermenting method to another. The English brewing company Charles Wells of Bedford, for example, describes its ale yeast as bottom-fermenting because it is used in a modern conical fermenter where it settles to the bottom of the vessel.

Yeast will react not only to the type of fermenting vessel used but also, crucially, to the variety of malt and to the temperature at which it is expected to work. Ales are fermented at higher temperatures than lagers and are also conditioned at warmer temperatures´ and the basic ingredient, the malt, will have different properties as a result of the strain of barley used and its handling at the malting stage.

Barley, in common with other cereals, is a descendant of the wild grasses used by early civilisations to make bread and beer. Barley is the preferred cereal for brewing because, during germination, the shoot is protected inside the grain while in other cereals such as wheat it breaks out of the grain and can be damaged.

Barley is easier to germinate and, during the mashing period when the starches are turned into sugar, the husks form a valuable filter to help the separation of the liquid wort from the spent grains.

The forms of barley used for brewing are maritime ones, grown near the sea in Britain and the Low Countries, and continental ones in central Europe. Some are winter barleys, hardy varieties planted in winter that can survive the cold and the frost; others

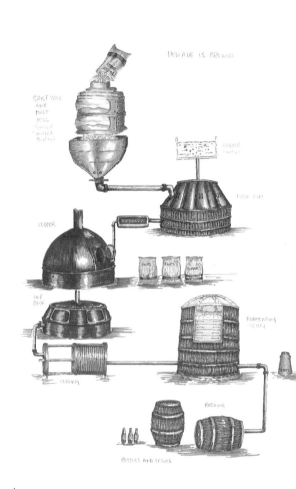

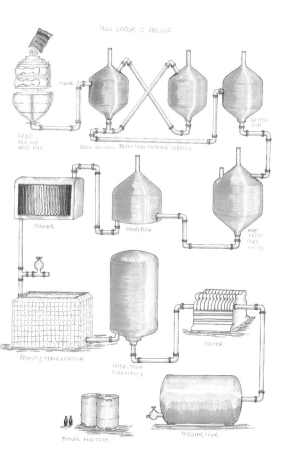

are spring varieties grown when winter is over. A classic English brewing barley, Maris Otter, is planted in winter. Lager brewers prefer spring barley.

Barley types may be two-row, four-row or six-row; rows refer to the number of the grains within each ear of barley. Two-row barley is grown principally in central and western Europe. Six-row tends to grow in warmer climates such as the Mediterranean, Australia and the USA. Four-row is confined to harsher, colder climates and, because of its high protein level, is not so suitable for brewing, though a micro-brewer on the islands of Orkney off the Scottish coast uses a four-row Neolithic variety to produce an organic beer.

What happens to the barley in the maltings determines not only the finished colour of the beer but also its taste characteristics. The grains are steeped in water in order to encourage germination, with the shoot growing inside the grain. When partial germination has taken place the grains are heated in a kiln. This stops germination and produces the type of malt needed by the brewer. Kilning at a comparatively low temperature produces a Pilsener or lager malt. The temperature is increased for the classic British pale ale malt, known on the mainland as Vienna malt. Higher temperatures produce crystal, caramel or Munich malt, used widely to give beers a copper colour. If the temperature is increased the resulting malts will be chocolate, black or roast; there is little fermentable sugar left in them but they add colour and a bitter, roasted character to beer.

Moisture content and temperature at the time of kilning determine the taste of beer as well as the colour. A lager malt will produce not just a pale golden beer but one with a delicate aroma and palate, too. Malt for ales has a more robust character as a result of the higher kilning. During the malting process the starch inside the grain has been transformed into maltose and dextrose. Maltose will form the main fermentable sugar that will be attacked by yeast and turned into alcohol, while dextrose adds flavour and body to beer.

The malt, biscuity to taste, is now ready for the complex brewing process. The first stage is mashing, where the malt is mixed with pure hot water – liquor

– to release the natural sugars. In classic ale brewing, a simple infusion mashing method, rather like making tea, is used. The mash tun is the teapot and the thick porridge-like mixture is left to stand for between one and three hours at a temperature of 65–68°C (149–154°F). When the brewer is satisfied that maximum conversion of the sugars has taken place the sweet liquid, called wort, is run through the slotted base of the tun and then the spent grains are sprayed or sparged with more hot liquor to wash out any remaining sugars.

British brewers claim that the infusion mash method is sufficient for them because of the superior quality of their maritime malt. The Continental decoction method evolved because, malt quality apart, the brewers believe that different enzymes are more efficient at different temperatures. As a result, mashing starts at a lower temperature of around 35°C (95°F) and lasts for up to six hours. Portions of the mash are pumped (decocted) to another vessel that has been heated to a higher temperature and then returned to the main mash until it has reached a temperature of 76°C (169°F). Depending on how often the mash is pumped from one vessel to another, it may be a single-decoction, double- or even triple-decoction mash.

When mashing is finished, the mixture is pumped to yet another vessel called a 'lauter tun' where rotating blades thin the mash so that the wort can leave through a slotted base. To complicate the matter, some brewers as will be seen in the main body of the book use a combination of infusion and decoction mashing known as step infusion. A few lager brewers use a simple infusion mash.

In both ale and lager brewing, the sweet wort is now pumped to a copper or brew kettle where it is boiled with hops. The hop plant (*humulus lupulus*, from *lupus* the wolf, because of the plants propensity to grow wild) is a member of the nettle and cannabis family. Its cone or blossom contains tannins, resins and oils that act as a preservative in beer, warding off infections, as well as adding essential bitterness.

Before the adoption of the hop, brewers used juniper berries or such plants as rosemary, myrtle and the hops close relation, the nettle, to add bitterness to beer. The hop was first used in the eighth and ninth centuries in Europe but did not arrive in England, via Flanders, until the fifteenth century.

Hops can be added to the wort as whole blossoms, as compressed pellets, or – rarely in quality brews – as a liquid hop extract. It is not usual to pour in all the hops at the start of the boiling process. They are added in stages and many brewers use hops with the greatest bitterness during the early stage and add aroma hops at the end so that the finished beer has a fine resiny, peppery appeal. There are many varieties of hops, and more are being introduced as growers tackle the problems of attacks from pests. On mainland Europe, the German Hallertau region is famous for its hops, as are the Saaz area of Czechoslovakia, and Slovenia in Yugoslavia. In England, Kent and Hereford & Worcester are the main hop-growing regions. All hops used in brewing are the female plants; hops intended for lager brewing are unfertilised – the male hop is vigorously hunted down and exterminated – while ale hops are encouraged to germinate in order to impart a more robust aroma to the beer.

The boil lasts for 60 or 90 minutes. The copper may have a slotted base if whole hops are used, with the spent blossoms acting as a filter as the wort runs out, or the wort may be pumped to a whirlpool where centrifugal force separates solids and liquid. The hopped wort is now cooled in preparation for its violent confrontation with yeast.

In the fermenting vessel – sometimes an open square or, in high-tech breweries, a closed vessel – an ale yeast will work with great rapidity at a temperature of between 15 and 25 °C (59–77 °F). Within 24 hours a heaving crust of yellow-white, with brown and black protein streaks, builds on top of the wort. The head of yeast is removed to allow the wort to breathe and, as the sugars turn to alcohol, the satiated yeast will finally surrender and drop to the bottom of the vessel. The process lasts between five and seven days. The rough or green beer will be pumped to a conditioning tank for a few days where it purges itself of unwanted aromas and tastes.

In a classic cask-conditioned ale, the beer will not be filtered but will be racked into casks, primed with sugar, given added aroma hops and left in the pub cellar to undergo a secondary fermentation. If a beer is conditioned in the bottle, as is often the case in Belgium, then priming sugar is added to encourage a second fermentation. Most of the British ales for export featured in this book are filtered and pasteurised, though a few are bottle-conditioned.

Lager brewing is a child of the industrial revolution, but for centuries brewers in hot climates had attempted to tackle the problem of their brews going sour during the summer. Their solution was to condition the beers in deep, icy caves where they noticed that the yeast sank to the bottom of the vessels but continued to turn sugars into alcohol. With the aid of temperature control, refrigeration and scientific yeast propagation in the nineteenth century, the pioneering Munich brewer, Sedlmayr, was able to turn a hit-and-miss form of fermentation into a wholly new method of producing beer.

There are two stages to the lager fermentation cycle. Primary fermentation begins at 5°C (41°F), rises to 9°C (48°F), and then falls back to the starting temperature. Contrary to expectation, if primary fermentation takes place in an open vessel a large head of yeast develops on top of the wort as with ale, but it does so more slowly as a result of the lower temperature.

Primary fermentation lasts for up to three weeks. The wort is then pumped to the conditioning or lager tank (from the German word for store, *Lager*) where it is stored at freezing point or just above. A secondary fermentation takes place as the yeast, at the bottom of the vessel, turns sugar into alcohol and carbon dioxide. The fermentation may be encouraged by adding some partially fermented wort; this is known as *kräusening*. The length of lagering will depend upon a number of factors such as the strength of the beer and the commercial pressures on the brewer to get the beer out into the trade. Conditioning periods are now falling, with the result that some beers lack the rounded balance of a true lager beer. Three weeks is the absolute minimum. The original pale Pilseners in Czechoslovakia enjoy 90 days. Strong beers may get many months or even a years conditioning.

When the lagering period is finished, the beer will be filtered to remove the solids that have built up in the conditioning tank. It will then be casked or bottled and may be pasteurised. Pasteurisation is a much-debated subject. Louis Pasteurs work in identifying the bugs that can cause brewing to be ruined was of crucial importance. His method of heating beer to stabilise it, however, was not so beneficial. Strong beers and stouts can survive it largely unscathed but lower gravity beers often leave the pasteuriser with a toffee, buttery or sugared almond aroma and palate that detract from the quality of the drink.

The argument in favour is a simple one: the beer will survive better in commercial outlets. To those who support that theory I recommend the views of the Brand brewery in the Netherlands: see the relevant entry.

Cereal adjuncts are equally controversial. Purists would prefer all brewers to follow the German 'Purity Pledge', the *Reinheitsgebot*, and use only malt, hops, yeast and water. Wheat, maize and rice are commonly-used adjuncts while brewing sugar or glucose is added at the boiling stage. They are not necessarily cheaper. Brewers who use them argue that they help counter any protein haze found in an all-malt beer. A leading and highly-respected English brewer, whose beers have won awards for their quality, said the use of adjuncts helped him 'to play tunes' with the palate of his brews. His customers seem happy with the melodies he composes. The debate will rumble on in these green and health-conscious times. It is a useful debate but it will be important to distinguish between ales and lagers and not to seek to place both styles within the same strait-jacket.

Using the guide

Brewers were all asked for the same information about their beers and responded in varying degrees. The strength of beer is represented by 'Alcohol by volume' (ABV), now being introduced throughout the countries of the European Community. 'Degrees Plato', an older German measure, is similar to the Czech 'degrees Balling' in common with the British 'original gravity' (OG), they are connected more with the gravity of the wort – the amount of fermentable sugars in solution – than with alcohol content. The ABV and OG are often similar – 3.6% ABV and

1036° OG, for example – but there can be differences depending on how far the beer is 'brewed out' to use up the sugar; if this is done efficiently, the beer will have a higher alcohol level than its OG would indicate.

'Units of bitterness' (EBU) is an agreed scale used by brewers to indicate the hop bitterness of the beer. Bitterness is not the same as dryness, which can come from the malt as well as the hops.

The tasting notes are mine, not the brewers. 'Nose' indicates the impact of the aroma of the beer – malty, fruity or hoppy. 'Palate' is the taste in the mouth, where the tongue recognises sweetness at the front, saltiness and sourness in the middle and bitterness at the back. 'Finish' is the lasting impression of the beer, the sensation left after the beer has disappeared down the throat; it may be malty, fruity, hoppy or a balance of all three.

Tasting beer

For a beer to be enjoyed to the full it should be agitated in the glass to release all the aromas. Surprisingly, perhaps, the aromas of some ales are slower to develop than those of lagers. The fruity notes of an ale appear as the beer warms up in the glass. The beer should have a lively head that leaves 'lace work' on the inside of the glass as the beer is drunk. Lack of head could be a sign of age or oxidation – or a poorly rinsed glass; detergents quickly kill the foam on beer. Let the beer trickle over the tongue, teasing out the malt, the fruit and the hop characteristics. Brewers have identified several hundred flavour elements in beer. You pay a tribute to their skill if you seek to determine those elements´ you also add to your own enjoyment and appreciation.

Temperature

All the skill of the brewer will be destroyed if the beer is served incorrectly. In a pub or bar, it is up to the bar staff and the cellarman to serve you a drink at the right temperature. At home, the task is down to you. Ales should not be served at room temperature, unless you live in an unheated house. The only exceptions to this rule are barley wines and beers of the Belgian monastic style. All other ales will benefit from about 15 to 20 minutes in a refrigerator. The ideal temperature for a British ale is 55°F (13°C). Lagers, whether light or dark, along with wheat beers, should be lightly chilled to 9°C (48°F). Do not follow the American and Australian custom of serving beers at 6°C, which masks the flavour.

GLOSSARY

Abbey beer: in Belgium and the Netherlands, commercially brewed beers based on the products of, or brewed under licence from, Trappist monastic breweries.

Adjunct: cereal added to the mashing process, such as maize, rice or wheat.

Ale: a beer brewed by top fermentation and warm conditioning, which usually has a pronounced fruity character. In Britain, ale is best expressed in its cask-conditioned or bottled-conditioned forms. There are many ales in Belgium, usually bottle conditioned.

Alpha acid: the bittering agent of the hop flower.

Altbier: 'Old beer' in German; a beer brewed by top fermentation, associated with Düsseldorf.

Barley wine: English term for a beer of high alcoholic strength. Usually served in small 'nip' bottles.

Berliner Weisse: the classic wheat beer of Berlin, often served with a dash of grenadine.

Bière de garde: the country beers of northern France, fruity and top fermenting. Literally 'beer to keep' or to lay down.

Bitter: the classic British pale ale, descendant of India Pale Ale.

Bock: a strong lager beer, usually brewed on a seasonal basis in spring, autumn or winter. Often dark, tawny or copper in colour but can also be pale. Stronger versions are known as *Doppelbocks*.

Bottle-conditioned: a beer that undergoes a secondary fermentation in the bottle, usually with the aid of a dosage of sugar.

Burtonise: to add salts to water in order to replicate the hard waters of Burton-on-Trent in England, rich in gypsum and ideal for brewing pale ale.

Caramel: roasted sugar added to give colour to beer. Outlawed in some European countries because of its E numbers.

Carbon dioxide: gas produced during fermentation

and vital to giving finished beer a good condition, sparkle and head. Applied carbonation can, however, make a beer unnaturally fizzy.

Cask: British term for a cylindrical traditional draught beer container which comes in several sizes; not to be confused with a pressurised keg which contains chilled and filtered beer.

Cask-conditioned: classic British draught beer which undergoes secondary fermentation in the cask.

Decoction: mashing system used in the lager brewing process.

Dortmunder beer associated with the German city, known as 'Dort' for short the term is also used in Belgium and the Netherlands. Dortmund is best known for its Export style beers.

Dunkel: German for a dark lager beer.

Export: a premium strength ale or lager. In Germany a beer that is stronger than a Pilsener.

Hefe: German for yeast. Indicates a sedimented beer, usually a wheat beer.

Helles or *Hell*: German for light or golden beer, the everyday beer.

Infusion: the mashing system used in ale brewing.

Kölsch: fruity ale associated with Cologne.

Kräussening: the system of adding partially fermented wort to a lager tank to encourage a strong second fermentation.

Lager: the German word for store. The conditioning stage of beers produced by bottom fermentation.

Lambic: Belgian beer produced by spontaneous fermentation. *Faro* is a sweet version, *Gueuze* a blended version, *Kriek* is lambic with cherries, *Frambosen* with raspberries.

Maibock: German beer brewed to herald the spring.

Märzen: German 'March beer', brewed in that month but stored until the Munich Oktoberfest.

Pilsener: also known as Pilsner or Pils, much abused term for the style of lager beers from Pilsen in Czechoslovakia. Today means a lager of any strength but should be a beer of around 5% ABV, with a good hop character and complex aroma.

Porter: dark, heavily hopped beer developed in London in the eighteenth century.

Reinheitsgebot: the Bavarian 'Purity Pledge' of 1516 that stipulates that only malt – barley or wheat – hops, yeast and water can be used in brewing. Now applies to the whole of Germany but non-Bavarian brewers are not bound by the Pledge in beers made for export.

Scotch ale: a strong malty ale originally from Scotland, exported to the Low Countries and also brewed there.

Stout: once the strongest porter beer in a brewery; now a dark, heavily hopped beer associated with Ireland, brewed from pale and roasted malt and usually some unmalted roasted barley.

Trappist: bottle-conditioned beers brewed by Trappist monks in Belgium and the Netherlands.

Urquell: German for original source; term applied to the Pilsener beer from Pilsen but too late to stop a million imitations.

Wheat beer: known as *Weisse, Weissbier* or *Weizenbier* in Germany. Beers brewed from a mixed mash of wheat malt and barley malt. Top-fermenting, fruity and sometimes slightly sour.

AUSTRIA

If countries that lose their empires have to discover a new role in the world then Austria also has to find its true brewing style. The small rump of the once mighty Austro-Hungarian empire lies in the shadow of the vast and reunited Germany and its beers seem to be in awe of the brews of Bavaria and the north. Austrian brewers now concentrate on golden lagers of the Pils type, yet Vienna in the nineteenth century developed its own distinctive beer style, and countries as far away as Mexico and Brazil produce beers in the Viennese fashion. In the mid-1800s, a brewer named Anton Dreher produced lager beers with an amber colour that resulted from the use of Vienna malt, which is cured more than the type used for a golden Pilsener. Dreher also worked closely with Sedlmayr of Munich to perfect the lager style of brewing which spread like a bush fire when refrigeration and yeast propagation were made possible by the technical innovations of the industrial revolution.

Influenced by nearby Munich, Austrian beers tend to be rounded, fruity and malty, but there is now a small trend back to producing Viennese beers with that characteristic amber or red touch of colour, while wheat beers are also coming back into fashion. Visitors to Vienna will find not only Pilsener in profusion but also stronger *spezials* and *starkbiers*, and even a genuine top-fermenting stout called Sir Henry's, produced by Baron Hendrik Bachofen von Echte in his brewery-cum-restaurant at Nüssdorf.

Although artificial colours and chemicals are not allowed, Austria does not lay down such a strict code as Bavaria's *Reinheitsgebot* or Purity Pledge. Adjuncts – mainly rice – are used, though some brewers proudly proclaim that their brews are all-malt and do adhere to the Purity Pledge of 1516.

Eggenberg
Brauerei Eggenberg, Stöhr & Co KG, Eggenberg
1, 4655 Vorchdorf

MacQueens Nessie Whisky
Malt Red Beer

ABV 7.5%; degrees Plato 17

Ingredients Imported Scotch whisky malt.
Hallertau hops. 26.7 units of bitterness. Bottom-
fermenting yeast.

TASTING NOTES

Nose Rich malt aroma with delicate hop notes.

Palate Powerful grain taste with a long smoky
finish – 'like a whisky and soda', the brewer says. It
has a fine amber colour.

Comments Eggenberg are not alone in using
whisky malt; Adelscott, brewed by Adelshoffen in
France, also includes malt to give it a delicious
smokiness in the finish. Eggenberg's version is not so
much an attempt to reintroduce a 'Viennese red' beer
as to establish a base in the European speciality beer
market. It is all-malt.

Draught version (unpasteurised) available in
France and Italy.
Bottled version (pasteurised) available in France,
Germany, Italy, Spain and Switzerland.

Urbock 23°

ABV 9.3%; degrees Plato 23

Ingredients Munich malt and Pilsener malt. Saaz and Hallertau hops. 40 units of bitterness. Bottom-fermenting yeast. Lagered for nine months.

TASTING NOTES

Nose Ripe fruity aroma with powerful dash of hop.

Palate Rounded balance of grain and hop with a long hoppy finish.

Comments A beautifully balanced beer and, because of the long conditioning period, light and refreshing despite the impressive strength. It is all-malt, golden in colour and comes in an impressive dark bottle.

Draught version (unpasteurised) available in France and Italy.

Bottled version (pasteurised) available in France, Germany, Italy, Spain and Switzerland.

Eggenberg is based in a castle and brewing dates back for several centuries.

Sigl
Josef Sigl Brauerei, A-5162 Obertrum SLBG

Weizen Gold

ABV 5.2%

Ingredients Pale malt and wheat malt. Austrian Hallertau hops. Top-fermenting yeast.

TASTING NOTES

Nose Fresh and inviting hop and cloves aromas.

Palate Refreshing in the mouth, gentle, lingering bitter-sweet finish.

Comments A quenching and fruity wheat beer, produced by a small independent family firm which claims it is the only one in Austria to adhere to the German Purity Pledge.

B ottled version (unpasteurised) available in Britain and Germany.

Steirerbräu
Steirische Bräuindustrie, Reininghausstrasse 1–7,
A-8020 Graz STMK

Gösser Export

ABV 5%; degrees Plato 12.2

Ingredients Pale malt, crystal malt, maize and rice.
Hallertau, Spalt and Styrian Aurora, Goldings and
Super Steirer hops. 20 units of bitterness. Double-
decoction mash. Bottom-fermenting yeast.
Conditioned for three to four weeks.

TASTING NOTES

Nose Rich malt and vanilla aromas with hop notes.

Palate Light toffee in the mouth, bitter-sweet finish
with creamy vanilla character.

Comments A rounded, malt-accented beer from a
large Austrian group that also produces a **Pilsener**
and a **Bock**.

Draught version (pasteurised) available in Cyprus,
Greece, Hungary, Italy and Liechtenstein.
 Bottled version (pasteurised) available in Britain,
Cyprus, Greece, Hungary, Italy, Liechtenstein,
Poland, Portugal, Sweden and Yugoslavia.

BELGIUM

Sales figures can be deceptive. Belgians quaff enormous quantities of Pilsener-style beers but the fact masks the growth of the small country's astonishing variety and diversity of other styles. There are beers with an ancestry that not only pre-dates lagering techniques but recalls the age before the hop plant was used and when country brewers allowed the yeast deposits in wooden vessels as well as any stray air-borne yeast to turn the sweet wort into alcohol.

Belgium's idiosyncratic beers are fortunately not hard to find in their home market and exports are growing fast. The Belgians take their beer with stolid seriousness and the brewers reply by promoting their specialities with zeal. Cafés and bars will offer beer menus while the house special or guest beer of the week may be chalked on a board. A connoisseur may call for many different varieties: a beer of the lambic and *gueuze* style – vinous, often cloudy, brewed by spontaneous fermentation; a cherry *kriek* or raspberry *framboise* – surprisingly refreshing and dry, as the fruit has been part of the brewing process; a 'white' wheat beer – cidery and quenching; a robust abbey or Trappist ale – ripe, fruity, produced either in monasteries or under licence from the monks; or a 'red beer' – slightly sour of palate and using well-cured Vienna malt.

Perhaps the most astonishing fact for the newcomer to Belgium and its beers is that, mass-marketed Pilsener aside, the beers of the country are brewed by the warm or top-fermenting method. Generically they belong to the same ale style as British cask-conditioned milds and bitters, and the beers share a robust fruitiness. However, the similarities in aroma and taste should not be exaggerated and even a Scotch Ale brewed in Belgium will be markedly different to the home-grown variety. One reason for the difference is strength. Until the 1980s, spirits could not be served in cafés and so powerful beers were brewed to make up for the lack of the 'hard stuff' on licensed premises. Sensibly the Belgians accompany strong beer with a meal; beer connoisseurs, such as Jan de Bruyne in his *'t Brugs Beertje*, Kemel Straat 5,

Bruges, will recommend how to marry good beer and food, as well as conducting tutored beer tastings.

Unlike British ales, Belgian speciality beers come mainly in bottled rather than draught form. They must be stored and poured with care, for they condition in the bottle, throwing a sediment. Many brewers now state on their labels the temperature at which their beers should be served and a small drawing indicates how bottle and glass should be positioned in order to leave the sediment behind.

Conscious of the great wine-growing nation to the south of them, Belgians designate their finest beers as *Grand Cru* or *Grande Réserve*. They stopper the bottles with wire-cradled corks and wrap them in tissue paper. This proper seriousness about beer is countered by a jovial approach to drinking by brewers and drinkers alike. They are aware that the patron saint of brewing is the thirteenth-century Flemish duke, Jan Primus, whose devotion to the fruit of the barley won him the title of 'King of Beer' and whose corrupted name of Gambrinus is remembered on bottle labels in Czechoslovakia and Germany as well as in Flanders.

Achouffe

Brasserie d'Achouffe, Rue du Village 32, 6666
Achouffe.

La Chouffe

ABV 8.5%; degrees Plato 19

Ingredients Pilsen malt, glucose sugar and spice.
Yugoslav Styrian, Czech Saaz and East Kent
Goldings hops. Top-fermenting yeast.

TASTING NOTES

Nose Spicy, estery with a powerful hop resin aroma.

Palate Rich balance of malt, spice and hop in the
mouth, intense bitter finish.

Comments Amber-coloured bottle-conditioned
beer brewed from spring water from the Ardennes
and the brewery's own yeast strain.

Draught version (unpasteurised) available in the
Netherlands.
Bottled version (unpasteurised) available in
France, Italy and the Netherlands.

Mc Chouffe

ABV 9.2%; degrees Plato 21

Ingredients Pilsen malt, brown candy sugar, honey and spice. Styrian and Goldings hops. Top-fermenting yeast.

TASTING NOTES

Nose Honey, woody aroma with strong hop notes.

Palate Ripe and fruity in the mouth, long finish with raisin fruit and hop bitterness.

Comments A dark amber bottle-conditioned beer that caters for the lovers of Scotch ale in Belgium.

Draught version (unpasteurised) available in the Netherlands.

Bottled version (unpasteurised) available in France, Italy and the Netherlands.

Both beers are in corked bottles. They are produced by two brothers-in-law who brewed as a hobby and gave up their jobs to become commercial brewers as a result of the popularity of their beers.

Achouffe is a small village in the Ardennes and the brewery is based on a farm.

ROSÉ DE GAMBRINUS

CANTILLON

BR. CANTILLON 1070 BRUXELLES
BIÈRE BELGE · BELGISCH BIER

FRAMBOZENLAMBIC
LAMBIC A LA FRAMBOISE

℮ 75 cl.
ALC. 5 % VOL.

Cantillon

Brasserie Cantillon SPRL, rue Gheude 56, 1070 Brussels

Gueuze

ABV 5%; degrees Plato 11.39

Ingredients Pale malt 65, wheat (raw grain) 35%. Kent Fuggles and Belgian Star hops (three years old). Spontaneous fermentation.

TASTING NOTES

Nose Light fruit and cider aroma.

Palate Dry and refreshing in the mouth, quenching fruity finish.

Comments Cantillon is one of the best renowned *gueuze* brewers in Belgium and the only one remaining in the Brussels area. It is based in the Gueuze Museum (open to the public; tel: 02 521 49 28). *Gueuze* is a blend of lambic beer and a mix of malted barley and wheat grain. Aged hops are used in large quantities as a preservative and the bitterness is therefore light. The wort is cooled in open vessels and is then fermented by micro-organisms in the tuns and the surrounding machinery. The fermented beer is allowed to age in cask for one to three years and is blended to produce *gueuze*, which is bottled and undergoes a secondary fermentation.

B ottled version (unpasteurised) available in France, Italy and the Netherlands.

Cantillon uses the lambic as a base for a full range of beers including *kriek*, where cherries are macerated in the beer for five to six months, and *framboise*, where raspberries undergo a similar maceration. The *framboise* or *frambozen* is a classic of its kind.

Chimay
Abbaye Notre-Dame de Scourmont, B-6483
Forges

Chimay Red

ABV 7%; degrees Plato 15.75; OG 1063°

Ingredients Not revealed but believed to be, for all
three beers, Pilsener malt and caramel malt from
winter barley, with some wheat in Chimay White. No
sugar. Hallertau hops and possibly American
Yakima. Spring water. Top-fermenting yeast.

TASTING NOTES

Nose Soft creamy vanilla aroma with good prickle of
hops.

Palate Gentle fruit and malt in the mouth, creamy
finish with underlying bitter hop notes.

Comments Copper-coloured bottle-conditioned ale,
brewed by Trappist monks in a monastery founded in
1850 close to the French border.

Chimay White

ABV 8%; degrees Plato 17.75; OG 1071°

Ingredients See Chimay Red.

TASTING NOTES

Nose Peppery hop and grain aroma.

Palate Fruit in the mouth, light dry finish with hop and sultana fruit notes.

Comments A paler beer than the red, refreshing and easy drinking despite the impressive strength.

Chimay Blue

ABV 9%; degrees Plato 19.62; OG 1081°

Ingredients See Chimay Red.

TASTING NOTES

Nose Gentle redcurrant fruit and hop aroma.

Palate Soft fruit in the mouth with lingering fruit and sherry notes.

Comments A memorable beer, as is the entire range. A version of Chimay Blue in a corked 75cl bottle is sold as **Grande Réserve**. The beers are known as the 'Burgundies of Belgium' and the Blue can be laid down for two to three years, developing a riper, port-wine character.

Bottled versions (unpasteurised) available in Britain, France and the Netherlands.
Chimay is the best known of Belgium's five monastic breweries and its products – including a cheese made with the beer – are widely available. The three Chimay beers are identified by the colour of their crown corks.

De Dolle Brouwers
De Dolle Brouwers, Roeselarestraat 12B, B-8160
Esen

Oerbier

ABV 7.5%; OG 1090°

Ingredients Munich malt, amber malt, torrefied malt, candy sugar, Belgian Spalt, Czech Saaz and Kent Goldings hops. 26 units of bitterness. Top-fermenting yeast.

TASTING NOTES

Nose Vinous, sultana aroma with peppery Goldings hop notes.

Palate Massive fruit in the mouth with a deep bitter-sweet sherry finish.

Comments Dark red-brown, complex beer. *Oerbier* means original beer, which is taken to mean a traditional craft brew in Belgium.

Arabier

ABV 8%; OG 1075°

Ingredients Munich malt, amber malt, torrefied malt, candy sugar. Belgian Spalt, Czech Saaz and East Kent Goldings hops. Top-fermenting yeast.

TASTING NOTES

Nose Intense apple and clove aroma, similar to a wheat beer.

Palate Fruit and hop in the mouth with enormous Goldings character in the dry, sultana finish.

Comments A pale beer, different in character from Oerbier, with a memorable hop character.

Bottled beer (unpasteurised) available in Britain, France and the Netherlands.

The label shows a parrot and the name of the beer is a complex Belgian joke imposssible to translate. 'De Dolle Brouwers' means the Mad Brewers. Joe and Kris Herteleer started to brew at home with a kit bought from Boots in England. They became literally mad about brewing and moved into a derelict brewery in Esen. The brothers also produce **Boskeun** (Easter Bunny) and **Stille Nacht** seasonal beers. The brewery is open to visitors (tel: 051 502781) where the brothers' mother conducts the tour with enormous enthusiasm and talk of 'savage hops'. 'Beer', she says, 'is made from malt, pure water, yeast and hops – they are all good for you, therefore beer is good for you'.

LUXE BIER VAN HOGE GISTING MET FIJNSTE MOUT EN HOP GEBROUWEN – GEWAARBORGD ZONDER SCHEIKUNDIGE PRODUKTEN

BIERE DE LUXE SUR LIE BRASSEE EN BELGIQUE AVEC LES MALTS ET HOUBLONS LES PLUS FINS ET SANS PRODUITS CHIMIQUES
OPDIENEN AAN 10° – 12° C   —   SERVIR A 10° – 12° C
HERGIST IN DE FLES – REFERMENTEE EN BOUTEILLE

Duvel
Brouwerij Moortgat NV, Breendonkdorp 58, 2659 Breendonk-Puurs

Duvel

ABV 8.5%; degrees Plato 17.5; OG 1070°

Ingredients Pale malt, brewing sugar for bottle fermentation. Saaz and Styrian hops. 30 units of bitterness. Top-fermenting yeast.

TASTING NOTES

Nose Enticing fruit and hop aroma.

Palate Ripe pear-like fruit in the mouth, complex finish with fruit giving way to hop bitterness.

Comments Duvel – pronounced 'doovul' – means devil and this wickedly strong beer can lead a drinker from the path of righteousness. To the unaware it looks, with its tempting pale colour, like a lager but this spicy top-fermenting, bottle-conditioned beer belongs to the ale school. It throws such a vast fluffy head when released from the bottle that Moortgat brewery supplies a special Duvel glass, like a giant brandy balloon, in order to contain beer and foam.

B ottled version (unpasteurised) available in Austria, Britain, France, Germany, Italy, the Netherlands, Spain and Switzerland.

Gouden Boom
NV Brouwerij De Gouden Boom, Langestraat 54,
B-8000 Brugge (Bruges)

Brugs Tarwebier/

Blanche de Bruges

ABV 5%; degrees Plato 11.3

Ingredients Pale malt, unmalted wheat. Belgian
and Styrian hops. 18 units of bitterness. Top-
fermenting yeast.

TASTING NOTES

Nose Spicy fruit and hop aroma.

Palate Light quenching palate with hop and citric
fruit in the finish.

Comments Splendidly refreshing wheat beer, pale,
cloudy with a dense foam. The brewery name means
'golden tree' and the bilingual label stands for 'white
[wheat] beer of Bruges'. "Our beers are more pure
than the Germans'!" the brewer said emphatically
when I asked if he adhered to the *Reinheitsgebot*.

B ottled version (pasteurised) available in Britain,
France, Italy, the Netherlands and Spain.

Brugse Tripel

ABV 9.5%; degrees Plato 21

Ingredients Pale malt. Belgian, Styrian and East Kent Goldings hops. 27 units of bitterness. Top-fermenting yeast.

TASTING NOTES

Nose Vast peppery Goldings aroma.

Palate Creamy vanilla in mouth, lingering tangerine fruit and hop in the finish.

Comments 'Tripel' is an indication of the strength of this sumptuous, ripe, hoppy pale brown ale.

B ottled version (pasteurised) available in Britain, France, Italy, the Netherlands and Spain.

Hoegaarden
De Kluis Brouwerij van Hoegaarden,
Stoopkensstraat 46, 3320 Hoegaarden

Hoegaarden White/
Witte van Hoegaarden

ABV 5%; degrees Plato 11.5

Ingredients 45% wheat, 5% oats, 50% malted barley. Coriander and curacao used for aromatic spiciness. Two hop varieties. 16.5 units of bitterness. Spring water. Top-fermenting yeast.

TASTING NOTES

Nose Spicy aroma with strong coriander notes.

Palate Orange and coriander in the mouth, light dry finish.

Comments Cloudy yellowish classic beer with great spice character, recalling the age before hops were used and spices were added to give bitterness to beer. Hops have a walk-on part in Hoegaarden White. A similarly spiced beer but using only barley malt and with a greater strength is bottled as **Grand Cru**.

Draught and bottled versions (unpasteurised) available in France, Italy, the Netherlands and Spain.

Forbidden Fruit/
De Verboden Frucht

ABV 9%; degrees Plato 19.5

Ingredients Malt. Challenger and Styrian hops.
Coriander spice. Spring water. Top-fermenting
yeast.

TASTING NOTES

Nose Spice and hop resin aroma.

Palate Soft and fruity in the mouth, deep dry finish
with hints of orange fruit, vanilla and hop.

Comments A superb claret-coloured strong ale that
makes a splendid digestif. Great aromatic appeal
from both the coriander and the generous use of
aromatic hops.

Bottled version (unpasteurised) available in
Britain, France, Italy, the Netherlands and
Spain. Hoegaarden, financially supported by the
Interbrew (Stella Artois) group, produces an abbey-
style **Benedict** (7.3%) and a perilously strong, pale
Julius (8.7%). The brewery is in the Brabant region.
The sole remaining brewery in the town had become
derelict but brewing started again in 1965, producing
a classic Hoegaarden wheat beer. The brewery
moved to new premises in 1978 which were then
destroyed by fire. Heavy investment was needed to
build a new brewery and support came from
Interbrew.

Jupiler

Brasserie Piedboeuf, rue de Vise 253, 4500 Jupille sur Meuse

Jupiler

ABV 5.2%; degrees Plato 11.86; OG 1047°

Ingredients Pale malt and rice. Four varieties of hops. Units of bitterness 24.5. Double-decoction mash. Bottom-fermenting yeast. Conditioned for five to six weeks.

TASTING NOTES

Nose Good balance of hop and citric fruit.

Palate Soft, fruity, a hint of sulphur in the mouth, dry finish with slight fruitiness.

Comments Belgium's biggest selling Pilsener-style beer, with plenty of easy-drinking character. Jupiler is now a member of the Interbrew stable.

Draught and bottled versions (pasteurised) available in France and Italy.

Liefmans
Brouwerij Liefmans NV, Aalstraat 200, B-9700
Oudenaarde

Goudenband

ABV 5.2%; degrees Plato 12.5; OG 1052°

Ingredients Pale, crystal and chocolate malts,
torrefied barley, maize and caramel sugar. Czech
Saaz and English Whitbread Goldings Variety hops.
20 units of bitterness. Top-fermenting yeast.

TASTING NOTES

Nose Rich fruit and peppery hop aroma.

Palate Ripe fruit and chocolate in the mouth, dry,
slightly sour finish.

Comments A world classic: a brown ale of great
complexity owing to the variety of malts and hops
and a special yeast strain that imparts a slightly sour,
typically Belgian character. After a seven-day
fermentation the beer is conditioned for a year in the
brewery cellars. The beer can be laid down and will
improve with age. Six months old Goudenband is
macerated with local cherries to produce **Kriekbier**,
which is stored in the brewery for two years (7.1%
ABV).

B ottled versions (pasteurised) available in Britain,
France, Germany, the Netherlands and Spain.

FRAMBOZENBIER

Liefmans

Frambozenbier

ABV 5.2%; degrees Plato 12.8; OG 1053°

Ingredients Pale, crystal and chocolate malts, torrefied barley, maize and caramel sugar. Czech Saaz and English Whitbread Goldings hops. 19 units of bitterness. Top-fermenting yeast.

TASTING NOTES

Nose Powerful fruit and hop aroma.

Palate Raspberry fruit in the mouth, long sweet-and-sour finish.

Comments Regarded as Belgium's classic raspberry beer; like Goudenband, it can be laid down for several years. Liefman's brewery is more than 300 years old and its slow mashing, fermenting and conditioning techniques have not changed over the centuries. The craft brewery is run by Rose Blancquaert – 'Madame Rose' – and the lovingly made beers have bottles hand-wrapped in coloured tissue paper.

B ottled version (pasteurised) available in Britain, France, Germany, the Netherlands and Spain.

Orval
Brasserie d'Orval, Abbaye Notre Dame d'Orval,
Orval 218, B-6823 Villers-devant-Orval.

Orval

ABV 5.2–6%; degrees Plato 13.5; OG 1055°

Ingredients 86.5% pale malt (Beauce, Gratinais,
Unterfranken and Prisma), 13.5% caravienne malt,
white candy sugar (350 kg per brew). Hallertau and
Styrian hops; dry-hopped with East Kent Goldings.
40 units of bitterness. Spring water. Infusion mash;
top- and bottom-fermenting yeasts.

TASTING NOTES

Nose Intense peppery hop aroma.

Palate Bitter gooseberry fruit in the mouth, deep
dry finish with enormous bitter fruit and hop
character.

Comments This is the beer that hops were
invented for. It is brewed in a 900-year-old Trappist
monastery near the Luxembourg border. The
brothers' beer is one of the worlds greatest, a
stunningly complex brew as a result of the use of
four malts and candy sugar that combine to give it an
orange colour, generous hopping that imparts a tart
bitterness, and a yeast strain that adds a touch of
acidity. The same yeast strain is used for primary
and secondary fermentation; the beer is then run into

club-shaped bottles and primed with sugar; a bottom-fermenting yeast completes the third fermentation. The beer can be laid down for two to three years; great care must be taken when pouring as it throws a heavy sediment.

B ottled version (unpasteurised) available in Britain, France, Germany and the Netherlands.

The name Orval comes from *Val d'Or* the golden valley. The label shows a fish with a ring in its mouth; according to legend, in the eleventh century the Countess Matilda, Duchess of Tuscany, dropped a ring in the monastery well. A trout came to the surface with the ring in its mouth and the delighted countess dubbed the area the Val d'Or.

Rodenbach
Brouwerij Rodenbach NV, Spanjestraat 133–141,
B-8800 Roeselare

Rodenbach

ABV 5.1%; degrees Plato 11.75; OG 1047.5°

Ingredients Pale ale malt, caramunich malt
[Vienna malt] and maize grits. Brewers Gold hops. 14
units of bitterness. Top-fermenting yeast.

TASTING NOTES

Nose Powerful sour and fruity aroma.

Palate Ripe fruit in the mouth, long bitter and sour
finish.

Comments An exceptional colour, aroma and
palate derive from the use of 'red' Vienna malt and
an ageing process in vast oak vessels where natural
micro-biological organisms add a sourness to the
beer. The beer has a double-decoction mash;
following primary and secondary fermentation the
beer is aged for at least five to six weeks and this
young beer is blended with old beer than has been
stored for up to two years. Some of the old beer is
bottled as **Grand Cru** (6.7% ABV) and is so tart and
sour that some drinkers add a dose of grenadine.

B ottled version (pasteurised) available in Britain,
France, Luxembourg, the Netherlands and Spain.

Westmalle
Abbdij der Trappisten Westmalle, B-2140 Malle

Westmalle Dubbel

ABV 6.5%; degrees Plato 16; OG 1064°

Ingredients Pilsener malt, candy sugar. English Fuggles, German varieties and Czech Saaz hops. Top-fermenting yeast.

TASTING NOTES

Nose Massive peppery hop aroma and fruit notes.

Palate Great hop and malt attack in the mouth. Lingering dry finish with fruit notes.

Comments The monks brew a 4.25% beer for their own consumption. It is pale in colour whereas the commercial Dubbel is amber in tone because of the use of darker malts and sugar. It is a wonderfully ripe and complex beer, the benchmark for other 'double' beers in Belgium. The brothers also produce a **Tripel** (8%). Beer has been brewed in the abbey of Our Lady of the Sacred Heart for more than 150 years and the monks also produce a local cheese, *Westmalle Trappistenkaas*.

B ottled version (unpasteurised) available in Britain, France and the Netherlands.

CZECHOSLOVAKIA

Czech brewers will claim they are responsible for one of the great beer styles of the world: Pilsener. The nation of Czechoslovakia did not exist when the first golden lager beer was produced in the mid-nineteenth century, for it was Bohemia that was home to the beer that revolutionised brewing techniques and consumer demand, but it would be churlish to deny modern Czechoslovakia, free at last from foreign occupation and sclerotic dictatorship, its place in the bibulous hall of fame. Bohemia was a major brewing region for centuries and the beers in and around the town of Budweis (its Germanic name; today it is called Ceské Budejovice) achieved such fame that they were supplied to the Bohemian court and were dubbed the 'Beer of Kings'. Beers from Budweis became known simply and generically as Budweiser beers, a tag used to great effect by the American Anheuser-Busch brewing corporation whose Budweiser – called the 'King of Beers' – is now the world's leading brand. The confusion between Czech and American Budweisers has led to several protracted legal battles. The two companies are now attempting to reach agreement on copyright of the names.

Bohemia was able to produce beers of great quality as a result of its fine malting barley, its aromatic Zatec hops (Saaz in German) and its pure soft water. But the innkeepers of Pilsen were not satisfied with the local offerings and set up a municipal co-operative brewery to supply their needs. The result in 1842 was the first pale golden lager beer. Lagering of beer had existed for centuries on a rough and ready basis, storing beer in ice-filled cellars or caves to undergo a slow conditioning. Refrigeration, yeast cultivation and propagation, and brewing free from attack from wild micro-organisms came with the industrial revolution and hastened a move towards a greater scientific control of beer production.

Middle European countries with long, hot summers needed beers that would both quench the thirst and survive the heat. Lagering on a commercial scale was developed in Munich but the beers were still dark in colour. It was the co-operative innkeepers in Pilsen who, by chance or design, startled first their customers and then the whole world with a beer that was marvellous to behold and to drink.

The Bohemians have been less fortunate with their names. While the two Budweisers confuse the consumer, Pilsener, Pils and Pilsner are the most abused beer terms in the world, spawning a variety of brews that have little in common with the original apart from their colour. The Pilsen brewery added *Urquell*, meaning original source, but non-German-speakers fail to grasp the connection and continue to drink thin, underhopped beers masquerading as the real thing.

Fortunately, a worldwide distribution and heightened consumer knowledge means that Pilsner Urquell is now receiving greater recognition. Budweiser Budvar is also exported with great zeal and has been followed by another Pilsen beer, Gambrinus. Others are likely to follow as Czechoslovakia opens itself to the west. For a small country it has a remarkable number of breweries, around 100, which flourished even under the old Stalinist regime. All Czech breweries remain under state control but the new government plans to hand them over to private ownership. The fear is that the need to attract investment could lead to some breweries being sold to western companies who are not likely to be impressed by the Czechs' 'uncommercial' dedication to all-malt beers that are locked away in conditioning tanks for several months. We can only hope that the western philosophy of 'brew it fast and move it out' will not prevail.

Budweiser
Budweiser Budvar, Karoliny Svetle 2, Ceské
Budejovice

Budweiser Budvar

ABV 5%; degrees Plato 12; OG 1049°

Ingredients Pale Pilsener malt. Czech Saatz hops.
20 units of bitterness. Spring water. Double-
decoction mash. Bottom-fermenting yeast.
Conditioned for three months.

TASTING NOTES

Nose Spritzy aroma of hops and gentle fruit.

Palate Quenching, beautifully balanced in the
mouth, bitter-sweet finish with light vanilla notes.

Comments A beer of enormous finesse whose
smooth drinkability results from the lengthy lagering
period as well as the careful use of ingredients that
allow the beer to be marketed in Germany as meeting
the requirements of the *Reinheitsgebot*. The Budvar
brewery was opened in 1895, by which time
Anheuser-Busch had been using the brand name
Budweiser for 20 years.

Draught version (pasteurised) available in Austria,
Britain, Germany, Italy, Spain and Switzerland.
Bottled version (pasteurised) available in Austria,
Belgium, Britain, Greece, Holland, Italy,
Luxembourg, the Netherlands, Poland, Spain,
Switzerland, USSR, Yugoslavia.

Gambrinus
State Enterprise of Plzen Breweries/Gambrinus,
U Prazdroje 304 97, Plzen [Pilsen]

Gambrinus

ABV 4.5–5%; degrees Plato 12; OG 1048°

Ingredients Pale Pilsener malt and brewing sugar
(sucrose). Saaz hops. 33 units of bitterness. Double-
decoction mash. Bottom-fermenting yeast.
Conditioned for six weeks.

TASTING NOTES

Nose Fresh hop and fruit aroma.

Palate Rounded grain and hop in the mouth, dry
hoppy finish.

Comments Gambrinus, cheek-by-jowl with the
Urquell brewery, should not stand in its shadow, for
it is a fine example of a hoppy Pilsener. It is different
in character, less fruity but more resolutely hoppy,
and the use of brewing sugar means that it is a
cheaper beer in its homeland.

Available in draught form (pasteurised) in
Germany, Hungary, Spain and Switzerland.
Available in bottled form (pasteurised) in Britain,
Hungary, Poland, Switzerland and USSR.

Pilsner Urquell
State Enterprise of Plzen Breweries/Plzensky
Prazdroj [Pilsner] Urquell, U Prazdroje 304 97,
Plzen [Pilsen].

Pilsner Urquell

ABV 4.3%; degrees Plato 12; OG 1048°

Ingredients Pale Pilsener malt. Czech Saaz hops.
40 units of bitterness. Triple-decoction mash.
Bottom-fermenting yeast. Conditioned for 70 days.

TASTING NOTES

Nose Enormous bouquet of malt, honey and hop
flowers.

Palate Complex, multi-layered balance of malt,
vanilla, hop. Deep finish with fruit, hops and spices.

Comments The aroma of this remarkable beer
comes bouncing and booming out of the glass or
bottle. Its complexity is as great as that of a fine
wine, moving between layers of bitterness and honey
sweetness. The brewing method is time-honoured:
primary fermentation takes place in small oak casks;
secondary fermentation in larger oak vessels in deep,
cold sandstone caves. Triple-decoction mashing and
generous hopping add to the stunning end product.

Draught version (pasteurised) available in
Belgium, Britain, Finland, France, Italy and the
Netherlands. Bottled version (pasteurised) in
Belgium, Britain, Denmark, Finland, France, Italy
and Spain.

DENMARK

Carlsberg is as synonymous with Denmark as the Little Mermaid. It is an international giant and, in common with Heineken, Löwenbräu and Stella Artois, has followed the path of licensing brewers in other countries to produce beers under its name. In its own country Carlsberg, which with Tuborg forms the dominant United Breweries, produces a range of interesting beers including the exceptional Gold. It seems sad that in other countries Carlsberg is best known for both some uninspiring light lagers and the sticky Special, which in Britain has encouraged others to emulate it with high gravity brews known as 'loony juice'. Perhaps to meet that criticism, Carlsberg is now moving more vigorously into the export market.

The group's importance to the development of modern brewing cannot be denied. Denmark was best known for its wheat beers until Jacob Christian Jacobsen, son of a brewer in Copenhagen, went to study in Munich under the great brewer Sedlmayr. Jacobsen was determined to brew using the new lagering techniques but knew he needed a bottom-fermenting yeast culture to do so. It is now part of brewing folklore that Jacobsen took two pots of Munich yeast back to Copenhagen by stagecoach, kept the pots safe under his hat and doused them with cold water at every stop along the way. Such was the success of his first brown lager that he built a new plant on a hill (*berg*) and named it after his son, Carl.

However, it was Tuborg, then a separate company, that pioneered pale lager beers in Denmark. Together the two companies launched pioneering work in yeast cultures that helped increase the understanding of fermentation and the development of stable and reliable beers. Today United Breweries own several subsidiaries, leaving a handful of smaller country breweries, mainly in Jutland, to take up the slack in the market. The most interesting of the independents, Faxe, is represented abroad by a canned beer with the unfortunate name of The Great Dane.

Carlsberg

Carlsberg Brewery, 100 Vesterfaelledvej DK
1799, Copenhagen

Elephant

ABV 7.5%; degrees Plato 15.9; OG 1065°

Ingredients Pale malt and sugar. Hallertau hops.
38 units of bitterness. Double-decoction mash.
Bottom-fermenting yeast.

TASTING NOTES

Nose Yeasty, grainy aroma with fruit notes
developing.

Palate Orange and tangerine fruit in the mouth, dry
finish with some hop character.

Comments A seductive pale gold colour leads into a
powerful but refreshing beer in which a basic fruitiness is offset by a good hop rate. The beer is named
after the impressive elephant gates at the entrance to
the Copenhagen brewery, one of the finest in the
world. Other companies are cashing in on the success
of Elephant with similar-strength beers: one is called
Giraf. Derogatory names for poor beer should
prevent the use of Horse, Camel and Gnat.

B ottled version (pasteurised) is available in
Belgium, Britain, France, Germany, Italy and
Poland.

ENGLAND

Burton upon Trent is to pale ale what Pilsen is to lager. The small Staffordshire town in the English Midlands developed a beer style in the late eighteenth and nineteenth centuries that was once sought after throughout the world. Pale ale, or bitter as it is more commonly known today, has retreated to its country of origin and even there is under attack by heavily advertised and lacklustre lagers. Fortunately, thanks to the activities of the vigilantes of the Campaign for Real Ale and a genuine sea-change in consumer preference, sales of bitter in its cask-conditioned form are now growing again. Before the Burton revolution, brewers produced brown beers; the style of dark porters and stouts, pioneered in London, swept the British Isles and were exported as far afield as the American colonies and the Baltic states.

When the call for a light and refreshing beer came from the civil servants and troops in India, the Burton brewers responded with India Pale Ale, high in gravity and generously hopped to help it survive long sea journeys. While the gentle waters of Pilsen allowed the brewers there to produce their soft, smooth-textured lagers, it was the hard spring waters of Burton, rich in gypsum, that helped give the sharp, slightly sulphury note to pale ales.

The brewers were helped, too, by a fermentation method based on the 'union set', great oak casks linked by troughs and pipes. Visitors to Burton can see still the union system in all its glory at Marston's brewery. Fermentation begins in conventional open square vessels but the wort is transferred to the unions casks where it gushes up into troughs above and then returns to the casks. The system ensures that the vigorously fermenting wort is in constant contact with the yeast. The end result is a beer that undergoes a volcanic secondary fermentation in the cask in the pub cellar.

Bitter is now brewed throughout the country and without the aid of union sets, but brewers adjust their brewing liquor with salts to 'Burtonise' it and many use fermenting systems that are not dissimilar to the old Burton method. In Yorkshire, the stone square system is based on two-storeyed fermenting vessels where the wort rises up from the ground floor through a central hole into the top floor and returns, leaving a slurry of yeast behind. Others use a dropping system; after a few days of fermentation the wort is literally dropped from one set of vessels to others below, action that aerates the wort and creates a lively natural carbonation.

Whatever the system employed, the uniqueness of English bitter stems from its final conditioning in its cask in the pub cellar. The secondary fermentation there is aided by the use of priming sugars while dry hops are often added to impart a good resiny aroma. A careful cellarman will monitor the conditioning process by the use of soft and hard pegs of wood placed in the bungholes in the casks to control the escape of carbon dioxide.

Warm fermentation and a short secondary conditioning mean that cask ales are ready to drink in a fraction of the time of a genuine lager beer. Fruity esters that a lager brewer will purge are positively encouraged by a brewer in England. Depending on its gravity, an English ale may well offer aromas of apples, citric fruit, blackberry, gooseberry, sultana, raisin and banana, allied to a generous hop appeal from fertilised male strains, such as the Kent Fuggles and the Goldings grown in Kent and Hereford & Worcester.

Little or no cask beer is exported today. Bar managers in other countries understandably lack the experience of dealing with a beer that is like a precocious child. English ale is now represented abroad in filtered bottled and keg forms though a few of those listed are superb examples of bottle-conditioned beer. The growing appeal of English ale in such unlikely countries as Italy and Spain suggests that cask versions may start to follow, recalling the great days of brewing when Bass of Burton was the largest producer in the world.

Adnams
Adnams & Co, Sole Bay Brewery, Southwold,
Suffolk IP18 6JW

Adnams Bitter

ABV 3.6%; degrees Plato 9; OG 1036°

Ingredients Maris Otter pale ale malt, sugars and
caramel. No cereal adjuncts. Challenger, Fuggles
and Goldings hops. 30–35 units of bitterness.
Infusion mash. Top-fermenting yeast.

TASTING NOTES

Nose Hop and citric fruit aromas.

Palate Rich grain in the mouth underlaid by good
hop feel, long bitter-sweet finish with citric fruit and
hop resin notes.

Comments Suffolk is in the heart of the East
Anglian barley growing area and Adnams bitter
benefits from the use of fine maritime grain that
gives a ripe fruit character to beer. The brewery is in
a delightful Victorian seaside setting, close to an
inshore lighthouse. Its water used to come from a
natural spring under the sea. That is no longer used
but perhaps the proximity to the sea still gives the
beer a slightly salty flavour. Adnams are planning to
export the bitter in cask form to other European
countries: tel: 0502 722424 for further information.

B ottled version (pasteurised) available in Belgium,
France and the Netherlands.

Bass
Bass Brewing Ltd, 137 High Street, Burton upon
Trent, Staffs DE14 1JZ

Bass Export Pale Ale

ABV 5%; degrees Plato 12; OG 1048°

Ingredients Pale ale and crystal malts. Challenger,
Goldings and Northdown hops. Infusion mash. Top-
fermenting yeast.

TASTING NOTES

Nose Complex aromas of fruit, butterscotch and hop
resin.

Palate Pronounced maltiness in the mouth offset by
long delicate finish with light apple notes.

Comments A bottle of Bass, with its familiar red
triangle trade mark, is immortalised in Manet's
celebrated painting *The Bar* at the *Folies Bergères*.
The beer then was almost certainly bottle-
conditioned. Today's version is filtered and
pasteurised which removes the classic hint of sulphur
that is the hallmark of a Burton ale. It is nevertheless
a complex, rounded and lingeringly fruity ale of great
quality.

Draught version (pasteurised) available in France, Germany, Gibraltar, Italy, Portugal and Spain.
Bottled version (pasteurised) available in Andorra, France, Denmark, Finland, Germany, Gibraltar, Iceland, Italy, Netherlands, Spain and Switzerland.

Bass is Britain's biggest brewing group and its cask-conditioned **Draught Bass** (OG 1043°) is the leading premium ale in the UK. It also produces **Worthington White Shield** (OG 1051°), a world classic, bottle-conditioned and the descendant of the original India Pale Ale. Sadly Bass has dismantled its union system and now uses conventional open squares. Its Bass Museum in Burton offers a fascinating history of British beer and brewing.

Batemans
George Bateman & Son Ltd, Salem Bridge
Brewery, Wainfleet, Lincolnshire PE24 4JE

Bateman XXXB

ABV 4.8%; degrees Plato 12; OG 1048°

Ingredients Pale ale malt (87%), crystal malt (10%),
wheat (3%) and brewing sugar. Challenger and
Goldings whole hops. 42 units of bitterness. Top-
fermenting yeast.

TASTING NOTES

Nose Rich aromas of hop resin and jammy fruit.

Palate Ripe malt in the mouth, deep rounded finish
with sultana and vanilla notes.

Comments A complex premium bitter with a
generous hop rate produced by a small family-owned
company with a deep commitment to its community
and local pubs. XXXB has won many awards at the
CAMRA Great British Beer Festival, including the
Supreme Champion Beer of Britain accolade.

Victory Ale

ABV 6%; degrees Plato 14; OG 1056°

Ingredients Pale ale malt (90%), crystal malt (5%), wheat (5%) and brewing sugar. Challenger and Goldings whole hops. 36 units of bitterness. Top-fermenting yeast.

TASTING NOTES

Nose Luscious aromas of hop resin and orange and pear-drop fruit.

Palate Full malt in the mouth, intense finish with complex balance of hop bitterness, raisins and vanilla.

Comments A fine, mellow strong ale brewed to celebrate the brewery's victory against closure. In the 1980s some members of the Bateman family wanted to sell their shares, forcing chairman George Bateman to raise the cash to buy them out or face the demise of the business. With the active support of his wife Pat, son Stuart and daughter Jackie, George prevailed and the brewery has gone from strength to strength under their stewardship.

B ottled version (pasteurised) available in Belgium, France and Spain.

Cornish
Cornish Brewery Co, Foundry Row, Redruth,
Cornwall TR10 8LA

Churchill Amber

ABV 5.1%; degrees Plato 13; OG 1052°

Ingredients Pale, crystal and amber malts, invert
sugar. Fuggles, Goldings and Progress hops. Double-
decoction mash. Top-fermenting yeast.

TASTING NOTES

Nose Peppery hop aroma and pear-drop fruitiness.

Palate Malt in the mouth, rich blackcurrant fruit
finish with good hop notes.

Comments The Cornish Brewery, part of the
Devenish group, produces a fine range of cask beer
and, under new management, has installed a
separate 'high-tech' brewhouse, with mash kettles
and lauter tuns, to concentrate on a large number of
speciality pot-stoppered bottles under the Newquay
Steam label. Churchill Amber is a well-crafted ale
that stresses the strong fruit character that is typical
of West Country beers.

Draught and bottled versions (pasteurised)
available in Italy.

Courage
Ashby House. 1 Bridge Street, Staines,
Middlesex TW18 4TP

Bulldog Strong Ale

ABV 6.3%; degrees Plato 17; OG 1068°

Ingredients Pale malt and brewing sugar. English hops; dry hopped with Styrians. Units of bitterness 42. Top-fermenting yeast.

TASTING NOTES

Nose Rich malt, peppery hop and some orange fruit.

Palate Pronounced hop on the tongue, long complex finish, bitter-sweet, becoming dry with fruit notes.

Comments Characterful strong ale first brewed for the Belgian market. It is warm-conditioned for a lengthy period to develop the rich and rounded palate.

Draught version (pasteurised) available in France and Italy.
Bottled version (pasteurised) available in Belgium, Denmark, France, Italy and the Netherlands.

Courage Imperial Russian Stout

ABV 10%; degrees Plato 25; OG 1102°

Ingredients Pale malt, amber malt, black malt and brewing sugar. Traditional English hops 'with hop rates four times that of average bitter' – indicating in the region of 24lb (11kg) of hops per barrel of stout. Top-fermenting yeast.

TASTING NOTES

Nose Fresh leather and peppery hop.

Palate Bitter black chocolate in the mouth with deep tart, bitter finish.

Comments This remarkable strong stout conditions in the bottle. It was first brewed by the Barclay Perkins brewery in London, which later became part of the Courage group. It is now brewed by the Courage subsidiary, John Smith of Tadcaster in Yorkshire. The stout acquired the 'Imperial Russian' tag as a result of its popularity at the Russian court when English brewers had substantial trade with the Baltic. To meet the demand, Barclay Perkins' shipper, Le Coq, built a stout brewery in Estonia, which was nationalised when the Bolsheviks came to power. It is brewed every three to four years and matured for many months in oak casks.

B ottle-conditioned version (unpasteurised) available in Belgium, Italy and the Netherlands.

Eldridge Pope
Eldridge Pope & Co PLC, Dorchester Brewery,
Weymouth Avenue, Dorchester, Dorset DT1 1QT

Royal Oak

ABV 4.8%; degrees Plato 12; OG 1048°

Ingredients Maris Otter pale ale malt, crystal malt
and brewing sugar. Fuggles and Styrian copper hops,
dry-hopped with Goldings. 30–35 units of bitterness.
Top-fermenting yeast.

TASTING NOTES

Nose Rich malt, hop and fruit aromas.

Palate Mouth-filling malt and fruit, long dry finish
with pronounced pear-drop flavour.

Comments A superb amber coloured and complex
ale brewed in a magnificent red-brick Victorian
brewery. The beer takes its name from the occasion
in the English Civil War when King Charles hid in an
oak tree to escape the parliamentary forces.

B ottled version (pasteurised) available in France
and Italy.

Goldie Barley Wine

ABV 8%; degrees Plato 22.5; OG 1090°

Ingredients Maris Otter pale ale malt and lager malt. Fuggles, Goldings and Styrian hops. 40–50 units of bitterness. Top-fermenting yeast.

TASTING NOTES

Nose Full malt and fruit with peppery hop notes.

Palate Warming malt in the mouth, massive fruit and hop finish with a good clean bitterness.

Comments A fine example of a classic English barley wine, its pale colour aided by the use of lager malt. It has a rich sherry-like character.

B ottled version (pasteurised) available in France and Italy.

Thomas Hardy's Ale

ABV 12%; degrees Plato 31; OG 1125°

Ingredients Maris Otter pale ale malt and crystal malt. Fuggles, Goldings and Styrian hops. 60–70 units of bitterness. Top fermenting yeast.

TASTING NOTES [From *The Mayor of Casterbridge*]

Nose 'Brisk as a volcano'.

Palate 'Full in body; piquant, yet without a twang; free from streakiness'.

Comments Thomas Hardy wrote with evident enthusiasm about the beer of "Casterbridge" (Dorchester) in his Wessex novels. Eldridge Pope have repaid the compliment with their classic bottle-conditioned beer named in his honour. It was brewed first in 1968 to mark the 40th anniversary of the writers death but interest and demand has meant that it is now brewed on a regular basis. It is dry-hopped and warm-conditioned for three months and is pitched three times with yeast, twice during fermentation and then during conditioning. It continues to condition in the small nip bottle and the brewery recommends that it is laid down for five years. A new vintage is brewed annually and each bottle is individually numbered. When opened there is a rich sherry or Madeira note beneath the intense peppery hop aroma. It is a remarkable example of British craft brewing.

Bottle-conditioned version (unpasteurised) available in France and Italy.

Fullers
Fuller, Smith & Turner PLC, Griffin Brewery,
Chiswick Lane South, London W4 2QB

London Pride

ABV 4.5%: degrees Plato 11.4; OG 1046°

Ingredients Pale ale malt and crystal malt, flaked maize, caramel and brewing sugar. Challenger, Northdown and Target hops. Top-fermenting yeast.

TASTING NOTES

Nose Ripe aromas of grain, hop and fruit.

Palate A multi-layered delight of malt and hops, a deep intense finish with hop and ripening fruit notes.

Comments First called Chiswick Pride, the ale became so popular in the metropolis that the name was changed in recognition of its wide appeal. Brewed in a handsome, ivy-clad Thames-side brewery, London Pride is a remarkably complex ale with massive hop and fruit character. The cask-conditioned version for the British market has a lower gravity of 1040° (ABV 4.1%).

ESB Export

ABV 6%; degrees Plato 14.8; OG 1060°

Ingredients Pale ale and crystal malt, flaked maize, caramel and brewing sugar. Challenger, Goldings, Northdown and Target hops. Top-fermenting yeast.

TASTING NOTES

Nose An explosion of malt, hops and marmalade fruit.

Palate Enormous fruit and hop in the mouth, strong Goldings character in the long finish with complex orange, lemon, gooseberry and tannin notes.

Comments Until micro brewers began to produce a range of strong premium bitters, ESB short for Extra Special Bitter was the most powerful of its breed in Britain (cask form OG 1054°, ABV 5.5°). It has a superb rounded balance of malty fruit and peppery hop, aided by the use of Goldings for aroma. ESB has won many awards in the Champion Beer of Britain competition.

Export contracts were being arranged with several European countries as the book was being completed. For up-to-date information contact Richard Fuller or Charles Williams on Tel: 081–994 3691.

George Gale

George Gale & Co Ltd, London Road, Horndean,
Portsmouth, Hants PO8 0DA.

HSB

ABV 4.6%; degrees Plato 12.39; OG 1050°

Ingredients Maris Otter pale malt, black malt,
torrefied wheat and glucose. Fuggles and Goldings
hops. 30 units of bitterness. Top-fermenting yeast.

TASTING NOTES

Nose Rich fruit and hop aromas.

Palate Malt in the mouth with a hop undercurrent,
intense finish with citric fruit and faint chocolate
notes from the black malt.

Comments Complex and distinctive beer, typical of
the brewery's fruity ales.

B ottled version (pasteurised) available in France
and Italy.

Nourishing Stout

ABV 5%; degrees Plato 11.9; OG 1048°

Ingredients Maris Otter pale malt, black malt, torrefied wheat, glucose and caramel. Challenger, Fuggles and Goldings hops. 22 units of bitterness. Top-fermenting yeast.

TASTING NOTES

Nose Malt and coffee aromas.

Palate Light toasted malt in the mouth, bitter-sweet finish becoming dry.

Comments A stout in the English tradition, sweeter than an Irish brew. It could not be called nourishing in the home market under British trade descriptions law. Before the crackdown, brewers produced milk stouts and oyster stouts, too.

B ottled version (pasteurised) available in France.

Strong Pale Ale

ABV 5.4%; degrees Plato 13; OG 1052°

Ingredients Maris Otter pale malt, black malt, torrefied wheat and glucose. Challenger, Fuggles and Goldings hops. 30 units of bitterness. Top-fermenting yeast.

TASTING NOTES

Nose Light malt and pear-drop aromas.

Palate Delicate fruit in the mouth, bitter-sweet fruity finish.

Comments A fruity and estery ale, a fine example of a premium English beer brewed by a staunchly independent family firm in Hampshire known to its supporters as 'George G. Ale'.

B ottled version (pasteurised) available in Italy.

Ind Coope
Ind Coope Burton Brewery Ltd, 107 Station Road,
Burton upon Trent, Staffs DE14 1BZ

Double Diamond

ABV 5.2%; OG 1053°

Ingredients Pale ale malt, crystal malt, chocolate malt, high maltose brewing sugar. Galena and Target hops. 35 units of bitterness. Top-fermenting yeast.

TASTING NOTES

Nose Rich fruit and hop aroma.

Palate Malt in the mouth, big finish with great hop character, refreshing for a beer of its gravity.

Comments A classic Burton pale ale with a hint of sulphur even in a filtered packaged version. Allsopp of Burton once vied with Bass and Worthington as the finest brewer of pale ale. It later merged with Ind Coope which in turn is now part of the giant Allied Breweries group. Double Diamond takes it name from the brewery habit of stamping its casks with diamonds to indicate the gravity of the beer: there were also Single and Triple Diamond beers. In Britain the DD recipe is used as the basis for the fine premium cask beer **Burton Ale**, winner of the Champion Beer of Britain award in 1990.

Draught and bottled versions (pasteurised) available in Italy, Spain and Sweden.

Nethergate

Nethergate Brewery Co Ltd, 11–13 High Street,
Clare, Suffolk CO10 8NY.

Old Growler

ABV 5.6%; OG 1055°

Ingredients Halycon pale ale malt, crystal malt,
chocolate malt. Fuggles and Whitbread Goldings
Variety hops. Top-fermenting yeast.

TASTING NOTES

Nose Light aromas at first, developing hop and
liquorice.

Palate Bitter-sweet in the mouth, deep finish with
hints of liquorice and black chocolate.

Comments A magnificent dark genuine porter,
brewed to a 1750s London recipe. Nethergate is a
micro-brewery in a picturesque Suffolk town. Old
Growler was launched by the England cricket
captain, Graham Gooch. When the team play badly,
Nethergate director Dick Burge says it is because
they forgot to drink Old Growler the night before:
cynics suggest the problem is just the reverse.

B ottled version (pasteurised) available in Austria,
Belgium and Italy.

Samuel Smith

Samuel Smith, The Old Brewery, Tadcaster,
North Yorkshire LS24 9SB

Old Brewery Pale Ale

ABV 5%; degrees Plato 12; OG 1048°

Ingredients Pale ale and crystal malt. Fuggles and
Goldings hops. 30 units of bitterness. Top-
fermenting yeast.

TASTING NOTES

Nose Rich malt and hop aromas.

Palate Complex balance of malt, light hop and fruit
with a grainy finish.

Comments A classic Yorkshire pale ale produced
by a remarkable and sturdily independent company.
Samuel Smith are great believers in traditional
methods and values: their beers for the home market
still condition in wooden vessels, they employ
resident coopers, and deliveries around Tadcaster
are made by horse-drawn drays. Pale Ale, fermented
in Yorkshire stone (slate) squares, is highly regarded
in the United States where it has won the Gold Star
award in the Los Angeles Times beer competition.
The judges described it as an 'outstanding brilliant
amber brew with inviting and complex aroma, rich
savours, traditional taste'.

B ottled version (pasteurised) available in France,
Germany and Italy.

Scottish & Newcastle
Scottish & Newcastle Breweries PLC, Tyne
Brewery, Gallowgate, Newcastle upon Tyne,
Tyne & Wear NE99 1RA

Newcastle Brown Ale

ABV 4.7%; degrees Plato 11; OG 1044°

Ingredients Pale ale malt, crystal malt, brewing
sugar, brewing syrup and caramel. Hallertau,
Northdown, Northern Brewer and Target hops.
Infusion mash. Top-fermenting yeast.

TASTING NOTES

Nose Malt and toffee aroma.

Palate Full bodied, malty and slightly sweet in the
mouth, pronounced toffee finish.

Comments Brown ale is a style unique to north-east
England: elsewhere in the country it indicates a low-
gravity bottled version of lightly-hopped mild ale.
But Samuel Smith of Tadcaster and Vaux of
Sunderland, as well as Scottish & Newcastle,
produce strong malt-accented, lightly-hopped brown
ales that are, perversely, a brilliant amber colour.
  Newcastle Brown for decades had a 'flat cap'
image until it became popular with students. In the
1980s it was promoted as a 'designer beer' alongside
the German Becks, which Scottish & Newcastle
market in Britain. Such is its fame that Newcastle
Brown is now exported to 40 countries and while it is

a classic bottled beer there is even a draught version for France. Scottish & Newcastle sell as much in the USA as they do in Britain.

Draught version (pasteurised) available in France. Bottled version (pasteurised) available in Bulgaria, Denmark, Finland, France, Gibraltar, Ireland, Italy, Luxembourg, the Netherlands, Portugal, Spain, Switzerland and Yugoslavia.

Charles Wells
Charles Wells Ltd, The Brewery, Havelock
Street, Bedford, Beds MK40 4LU

Bombardier

ABV 4.5%; degrees Plato 11; OG 1044°

Ingredients Pale ale malt, crystal malt, invert
sugar and caramel. Target copper hops, Goldings for
aroma. 36 units of bitterness. Bottom-fermenting
yeast*.

TASTING NOTES

Nose Rich, earthy hop resin bouquet.

Palate Ripe malt in the mouth with good hop
balance, intensely dry finish with blackcurrant notes.

Comments A deep copper-coloured ale with a rich
fruity character. Charles Wells moved from their
traditional Bedford brewery in the 1970s to a new
custom-built high-tech one with computer controls,
lauter tuns, whirlpools and conical fermenters. It
produces two distinctive and fruity cask beers, **Eagle
Bitter** (ABV 3.6%; OG 1035°) and a 1042° OG
version of Bombardier (ABV 4.2%). Bombardier is
an army rank. Charles Wells brews a strong bottled
beer called **Fargo**, much to the displeasure of the US
banking group Wells Fargo, which has a London
office. The brewery had to agree to withdraw a
draught version of the beer. Bombardier is fittingly

popular in Italy as there is a large Italian community in Bedford. The Italian version of the beer has a different specification: (ABV 5.4%; degrees Plato 13.5; OG 1054°.
The yeast strain used is an ale one that has adapted to conical fermenters.

Draught version (pasteurised) available in Italy. Bottled version (pasteurised) available in Italy and Germany.

FINLAND

Finland has a proud and remote brewing tradition that includes such local specialities as a beer brewed with barley and rye and flavoured with juniper berries. Its more conventional breweries produce not only lagers but a few top-fermenting ales and a superb porter called Koff, short for the name of the brewery, Sinebrychoff, founded by a Russian when the country was part of the Tzarist empire. The isolation of the country and the small number of brewers means that little beer is exported. If Sinebrychoff sold its ale in the USA it would surely be popular with television 'couch potatoes', for it is called Cheers.

Kulta
Oy Hartwall AB, PO Box 31, SF-00391 Helsinki

Kulta

ABV 5.3%; OG 1049°

Ingredients Pale malt and unmalted cereals.
Hallertau and Saaz hops. Bottom-fermenting yeast.
Conditioned for six months.

TASTING NOTES

Nose Light fruit and grain aroma.

Palate Rounded malt in the mouth, bitter-sweet
finish with delicate orange fruit notes.

Comments Kulta is called *Lapin Kulta* in Finland
and means Lapp Gold. The Lapin was dropped from
the export label in case people thought it had some
connection with rabbits. The brewery is in Lapland
and is one of the most northerly providers of beer in
the world. It was a small independent concern until
the large Hartwall group began to market it in
Helsinki where it became a cult beer and Hartwall
decided to buy the pot of gold. As well as home-
grown barley, the beer uses pure water from the
surrounding fjords. It is not only gold in colour but is
popular with gold prospecters in Lapland who stage
an annual drinking and gold-panning competition.

B ottled version (filtered but not pasteurised)
available in Britain and Switzerland.

FRANCE

France may seem an odd country to have a beer tradition. It is the worlds greatest – in terms of quality, not quantity – wine producer and the devotion to the grape would appear to leave little room for an appreciation of beer. But throughout the Latin countries there is a swing away from wine towards beer, which is perceived as a healthier drink. The problem for French beer drinkers is one that British consumers will readily understand, for France is dominated by a handful of giant groups producing some thin and uninspired lagers in the ersatz Pilsener style. In common with the large British brewers, the French giants also have a few quality beers but as always it is the small independents who wave the flag most vigorously.

The north-east region of Alsace, centred on Strasbourg, is the best-known brewing area of France but the influence is German as the brewing town of Schiltigheim and such companies as Fischer and Gruber stress. There are a few interesting lagers but in general they do not match the quality of the beers across the border. It was the president of Fischer who began the action that forced the European Court to declare the German *Reinheitsgebot* a 'restraint of trade', with the aim of flooding the vast German market with foreign beers brewed to lower standards.

North-west France is where the most fascinating beers are found. The Flanders region spreads from Belgium into France and breweries with names such as Duyck stress the Flemish connection while St Sylvestre calls its Trois Monts brand a *bière de Flandre*. That Flemish connection means that the beers of the *Pas de Calais* and *Département du Nord* are top-fermenting – *fermentation haute* – and form a style known as *bière de garde*. The style shows how over-simplified is the division of the beer world into ale and lager, for *bière de garde* means beer to be kept or stored: the Germans would say lagered. Traditionally a *bière de garde* would be conditioned in large oak casks for a month or so. *Bières de garde* form a distinctive regional style produced by country brewers using traditional methods.

Adelshoffen
Grande Brasserie Alsacienne d'Adelshoffen, 87
route de Bischwiller, 67300 Schiltigheim

Adelshoffen Export

ABV 4.5%; degrees Plato 11.2; OG 1044°

Ingredients Pale malt and maize. Hallertau and
Styrian hops. 18–22 units of bitterness. Bottom-
fermenting yeast. Conditioned for six to eight weeks.

TASTING NOTES

Nose Light, clean malty aroma with some citric fruit
notes and gentle hop character.

Palate Malt in the mouth, dry finish with some fruit
and hop notes.

Comments A quenching, lightly fruity beer lagered
for considerably longer that most mainstream French
lagers.

Bottled version (pasteurised) available in Britain,
Portugal, Spain and Switzerland.

Adelscott

ABV 6.6%; degrees Plato 16; OG 1065°

Ingredients Malt, whisky malt, and maize. Alsace Brewers Gold, Hallertau and Styrian hops. 16–20 units of bitterness. Bottom-fermenting yeast. Conditioned for six to eight weeks.

TASTING NOTES

Nose Delectable smoked malt aroma.

Palate Rich malt in the mouth, light smoky finish.

Comments A fascinating speciality lager with a clever brand name that cashes in on the French interest in 'le whisky'. Whether the malt is true peat-cured Scotch whisky malt or is carefully prepared in France, the end result is a beer with a delicious smoked character. Unconsciously, no doubt, the company is paying as much a tribute to the old German style of smoked beers – *Rauchbiers* – as it is to whisky.

Draught version (unpasteurised) available in Austria and Switzerland.
Bottled version (pasteurised) available in Austria, Belgium, Britain, Germany, Italy and Switzerland.

Duyck

Brasserie Duyck, Grande Rue, 59144 Jenlain

Jenlain Bière de Garde

ABV 6.3%; degrees Plato 16

Ingredients French Beauce, Brie and Gratinais malts. Flemish hops. 25 units of bitterness. Spring water. Top-fermenting yeast. Stored for one month.

TASTING NOTES

Nose Malt, fruit and peppery hop aromas.

Palate Rich malt in the mouth, bitter-sweet finish with liquorice notes.

Comments A classic *bière de garde*, amber coloured, a superb balance between malt, fruit and hops. After storing, the beer is filtered but not pasteurised and is sold in draught form in the Valenciennes area. It is an all-malt beer, including some roasted malt the brewery does not state the proportion. The bottled version is corked with a wire cradle. Jenlain is a village of 1000 people.

Bottled version (unpasteurised) available in Belgium and Britain.

The brewery was started by Felix Duyck, a farmer from Flanders, who in common with most farmers in the area brewed beer for his workers. His son, Robert, has considerably expanded and modernised the brewery inside the old farm buildings.

EMB:77030

75 cl e

BRASSÉE PAR G.B.G. FAUBOURG DE PARIS DOUAI POUR

LUTÈCE
Bière
de Paris

PUR MALT

PRODUCT
OF FRANCE

750 ml

PRODOTTA ED IMBOTTIGLIATA IN FRANCIA

LA BRASSERIE NOUVELLE DE LUTÈCE, PORT DE PARIS-94380-BONNEUIL

Lutèce

Brasserie Nouvelle de Lutèce, Port Autonome de
Paris, 15 rue du Moulin-Bateau, 94387 Bonneuil

Lutèce Bière de Paris

ABV 6.4%; degrees Plato 15

Ingredients Munich, crystal and caramel-amber
malts. Spalt and Saaz hops. 23 units of bitterness.
Bottom-fermenting yeast. Conditioned for 60 days.

TASTING NOTES

Nose Malt and fruit aromas.

Palate Malt, raisin fruit in the mouth, deep finish
with liquorice and chocolate notes.

Comments A rich amber-coloured beer in a
Burgundy-shaped bottle with a foil-wrapped neck
and beautifully designed label depicting medieval
Paris. Lutèce has been described as a *bière de garde*.
The style is similar but Lutèce uses a bottom-
fermenting yeast and is correctly designated a *bière
de Paris* even though it is now produced near Douai.
The name Lutèce is a corruption of Lutetia, the
Roman name for Paris. Brewing existed there in
Roman times and records show that 28 breweries
were still operating at the time of the Revolution.
The brewers were based in the area known as La
Glacière, fed by the waters of the river Bièvre,
named after the beavers that bred there.
   Brewing was seasonal and the beers were stored in

icy caves, which encouraged the development of a bottom-fermenting yeast strain. The beer style was known as *brune de Paris* – Paris brown – as a result of its amber colour. Lutèce was founded in 1920 on the site of the old *Brasserie de la Glacière* and while it has now left the capital it can claim to continue the old Parisian style.

Draught version (pasteurised) available in Italy and the Netherlands.

Bottled version (pasteurised) available in Italy, the Netherlands and Spain.

Meteor
Brasserie Meteor, 6 rue du Général Lebocq,
67270 Hochfelden

Meteor Pils

ABV 4.9%; degrees Plato 12.5

Ingredients Pale malt and corn grits. Czech Saaz
and Alsace hops. 35 units of bitterness. Bottom-
fermenting yeast. Single-decoction mash.
Conditioned for one month.

TASTING NOTES

Nose Toasty grain and hop aromas.

Palate Delicate grain and hop in the mouth, dry
finish with good hop character and honey notes.

Comments There has been a brewery in the village
of Hochfelden for centuries, supplying both an abbey
and local farms. The present brewery became a
commercial concern in the 1840s when it was bought
by a brewer from Strasbourg. Meteor Pils was
developed in the 1920s as a result of the explosive
popularity of the original Bohemian Pilsener. The
Czech government at the time attempted to bolt a
wide-open stable door by licensing the term 'Pils' and
entered into an agreement with Meteor for the use of
the name, the only such agreement in the French
brewing industry. Although Meteor is not an all-malt
beer and has a comparatively short conditioning

period, the honey notes in the finish are reminiscent of Pilsner Urquell.

Draught version (unpasteurised) available in Andorra, Belgium, Italy and Spain.

Bottled version (pasteurised) available in Andorra, Belgium, Britain, Italy, Portugal, Spain and Switzerland.

St Sylvestre

Brasserie de St Sylvestre, 1 rue de la Chappelle,
58114 St Sylvestre, Cappel

Trois Monts

ABV 8%; degrees Plato 19; OG 1080°

Ingredients Pilsener malt and brewing sugar.
Brewers Gold and Tettnang hops. Units of bitterness
27. Top-fermenting yeast.

TASTING NOTES

Nose Malt, fruit and light hop aromas.

Palate Rich malt in the mouth, long dry finish with
fruit, hop, coffee and liquorice notes.

Comments Trois Monts is labelled a *bière de
Flandre* and is a fine example of the style, complex,
rounded, well-balanced between malt and hop. The
rustic label shows a windmill against a background of
three hills.

Draught and bottled versions (unpasteurised)
available in Belgium, Italy and the Netherlands.

GERMANY

To the casual drinker Germany is *the* lager country.
It is true that the type of beer produced by cold
conditioning and bottom-fermenting yeast was
developed in Germany – or Bavaria to be precise –
but, outside breweries, the term is hardly used there.
To ask simply for a lager in a German bar could cause
confusion; you might even be shown the food store in
the kitchen. Germans, punctilious people, are as
careful as the British when ordering beer. Just as a
British drinker will call for a mild, a bitter, a stout –
or if he or she lacks discrimination – a lager, their
German counterparts will order by style and will
specify a *Helles*, a *Dunkel*, a *Pils* or an *Export*. At
certain times of the year they may demand a
Märzenbier – a March beer – or a strong *Bock*.
Around Düsseldorf they will order an *Altbier*,
literally an 'old beer', brewed by top fermentation.
Cologne, too, has top-fermenting golden Kölsch
beers, while there is a growing national demand for
wheat beers, also made in the old fashion that pre-
dates lagering. In Bavaria, wheat beers are cidery
and refreshing; in Berlin, so tart that many drinkers
add grenadine to take the edge off the sourness.

In other words, Germany is a country of variety;
and to match that demand it has a vast number of
breweries. Although numbers have been falling fast,
there are still some 1200 breweries in the old western
part of the country, 800 of them in the remarkable
state of Bavaria where every village seems to boast
its own tiny brewhouse and many monasteries still
chip in with distinctive contributions. Not
surprisingly, Germans are the greatest beer drinkers
in the world. The average German consumes around
150 litres a year while the Bavarians knock back 240.
The German Democratic Republic used to come
second in the consumption stakes and will now be
swelling the total for the whole of united Germany.

Only a small minority of German brewers export
their beers – the term Export in Germany describes a
style and strength of beer rather than a statement of
intent – as their time is taken up with meeting local
demand. There are none at all featured here from the
old eastern section. Either side of shotgun
unification, breweries in the east were falling like

drunks after an all-night session. They were said to be 'old-fashioned' and 'out of date', often the commercial view of quality and tradition. They were no match for western breweries with their marketing and PR teams anxious to soak up the formerly untapped reservoir of beer drinkers in the GDR.

One thing the GDR certainly lacked was the *Reinheitsgebot*, Western Germany's purity law. The Purity Pledge dates from 1516 and was confined to Bavaria until the first all-German republic was formed in 1919. The Bavarians joined the republic on the clear understanding that the *Reinheitsgebot* would cover all breweries. The Pledge was introduced in the sixteenth century by Duke Wilhelm IV who stipulated that only malt, yeast, hops and water could be used in brewing. His aim was not altruistic as he held a monopoly in the supply of brewing malt, but over the centuries the Pledge has prevented the adulteration or cheapening of beer with inferior ingredients such as sugar, rice, corn starch and even pasta flour as well as the great raft of chemical additives used in modern times to give beers a fake sparkle and great longevity. Germans today speak scathingly of the 'chemi-beers' produced in other countries.

In 1987 the European Court was lobbied by brewers outside Germany to declare the Purity Pledge illegal. Until then, beers that did not meet the strictures of the Pledge could not be sold in the Federal Republic. The court ruled in favour of the lobbyists and a law that should be a benchmark for quality was absurdly labelled a 'restraint of trade'. The Germans rallied to their pure beers. Brewers labelled their products 'brewed according to the *Reinheitsgebot*' and put plaques to this effect outside their breweries. To date there has been little penetration of the vast German beer market by foreign companies.

Cynics – and the beer world seems to have more than its fair share – claim that German brewers may use only malt, yeast and hops in their beers but this does not prevent them treating their water in order to overcome some of the problems of brewing from pure ingredients. There have been several scandals in recent years involving brewers who transgressed the Purity Pledge and one culprit made the supreme sacrifice by committing suicide. But most brewers remain loyal to the Pledge for the simple reason that it is the way they have always brewed. They have no desire to change their recipes and, above all, they are proud of their products. As any regular visitor to Germany knows, the beers *taste* clean and even over-indulgence does not lead to that dreadful feeling of incapacity of brain and limbs caused by a non-German hangover.

There is one loophole in the *Reinheitsgebot* that is of importance to this book: only Bavaria brews its beer for export according to the legislation. Brewers in other parts of Germany can exempt themselves, which means that beers in the export market may have the type of chemical pit-props used by less discriminating brewers throughout the world. Companies that are loyal to the Purity Pledge usually make this clear on their bottle labels.

Most beers sold for export are of the Pilsener type. The everyday beers – *Helles*, meaning light, or *Dunkel*, meaning dark – are reserved for home consumption, as are such local specialities as the top-fermenting beers, though wheat beers are finding a growing market in other European countries. Faced by such a galaxy of fine golden lager beers, it may startle the uninitiated to learn that, while lagering was developed in the Munich area, the first lagers were dark. With the aid of refrigeration, the innovative Munich brewer Gabriel Sedlmayr began in the 1820s to experiment with the technique of cold conditioning and bottom-fermenting yeasts. The first golden lager was perfected in neighbouring Bohemia and it was not until the 1950s that light beers become more popular than dark ones in Germany – mirroring the situation in Britain, where pale ale replaced mild as the preferred style.

German beers should be drunk and admired for their purity, their range, their variety and, above all, their quality. It is heartening to drink beers produced by people who take painstaking pride in their work.

Aying
Brauerei Aying, Frank Inselkammer KG,
Zornedinger Strasse 1. D-8011 Aying

Bräu Weisse

ABV 5.1%; degrees Plato 12.2; OG 1049°

Ingredients Pale malt and wheat malt. Hallertau,
Spalt and Hersbrcker hops. 15 units of bitterness.
Top-fermenting yeast. Conditioned for one month.

TASTING NOTES

Nose Enticing estery aroma with hints of apple and
cloves.

Palate Tart in the mouth with a deep refreshing
finish and lingering fruit notes.

Comments A superb wheat beer, pale in colour and
with a spritzy Champagne sparkle in the glass and
mouth. The sediment from the previous brew is used
as the fermenting agent. Locals traditionally drink it
with a twist of lemon.

Jahrhundertbier

ABV 5.5%; degrees Plato 13.2; OG 1053°

Ingredients Pale malt. Hallertau, Saaz, Spalt and Hersbrücker hops. 25 units of bitterness. Bottom-fermenting yeast. Conditioned for two months.

TASTING NOTES

Nose Massive herbal hop bouquet.

Palate Soft, rounded malt and hops in the mouth, long finish with bitter hop notes.

Comments As the hop varieties suggest, the pale golden beer – first brewed to mark a centenary celebration – as a massive hop resin aroma and finish.

Draught and bottled versions (unpasteurised) are available in France and Italy.

British readers should note that Ayingerbräu draught beers are brewed under licence by Samuel Smith.

The Aying brewery is in a handsome village in superb Bavarian countryside. The Inselkammer family have been innkeepers and brewers in the village for generations and pride themselves on the quality of their beer, none of which is pasteurised. They also produce a copper-coloured **Ur-Weisse** wheat beer, **Maibockbf**, **Marzen** and a powerful double bock called **Celebrator**.

Bitburger
Bitburger Brauerei Th Simon, D-5520
Bitburg/Eifel

Bitburger Pils

ABV 4.6%; degrees Plato 11.3; OG 1043-46°

Ingredients Alexis, Arena and Steiner pale malts.
Hersbrücker, Hüller, Perle and Tettnang hops.
Bottom-fermenting yeast. Conditioned for three
months.

TASTING NOTES

Nose Light hop aroma.

Palate Dry malt and delicate hop in the mouth,
exceptionally dry finish.

Comments Bitburger, which takes it name from the
town of Bitburg in the Rhineland, derives its dryness
from a full attenuation during fermentation that
leaves little sugar in the beer. The delicate aroma and
palate derive from a lengthy lagering period. The
company has a vigorous and aggressive approach to
marketing that has made the brand famous
internationally with the slogan 'Bitte ein Bit' – 'a Bit,
please'. It sells more than seven million hectolitres a
year from a modern high-tech brewery.

Draught and bottled versions (unpasteurised)
available in Austria, Belgium, Britain, France,
Italy, Luxembourg, the Netherlands and Spain.

DAB

Dortmunder Actien-Brauerei AG, Steigerstrasse
20, D-4600 Dortmund 1

DAB Original

ABV 5%; OG 1047

Ingredients Pale malt. Hallertau Northern Brewer
hops. 27–31 units of bitterness. Single-decoction
mash. Bottom-fermenting yeast. Conditioned for two
months.

TASTING NOTES

Nose Malty 'puffed wheat' aroma with light citric
notes.

Palate Clean and refreshing in the mouth, intense
bitter finish with lemon fruit.

Comments A fine example of a Dortmunder beer,
from one of the great brewing cities of Germany,
home to seven commercial producers, of which DAB
is the biggest. A 'Dort' is a style of lager brewing in
its own right, distinctively malty but drier than a
Munich beer. The brewers of Dortmund switched to
lager brewing in the late nineteenth century and had
to meet the enormous demand from manual workers
in the areas mining and steel industries. The generic
Dortmunder style became so popular throughout
Germany that it became known as Export. Today the
Dortmund brewers, conscious of middle-class

expectations and concern with image, give less
prominence to Export and its cloth cap antecedents
and concentrate on marketing Pilseners.

Draught version (unpasteurised) available in
Austria, Belgium, Greece, Italy, the
Netherlands, Spain and Switzerland.
   Bottled version (pasteurised) available in Austria,
Belgium, Britain, Czechoslovakia, Finland, France,
Greece, Hungary, Italy, Luxembourg, the
Netherlands, Norway, Poland, Romania, Sweden and
Switzerland.

DUB
Dortmunder Union Brauerei AG, Rheinische
Strasse 2, D-4600 Dortmund 1

Siegel Pils

ABV 5%; degrees Plato 11.4; OG 1046°

Ingredients bf Pale malt. Hallertau hops. 30 units of
bitterness. Double-decoction mash. Bottom-
fermenting yeast. Conditioned for six to eight weeks.

TASTING NOTES

Nose Rich aroma of malt with some hop hints.

Palate Light malt in the mouth, dry finish with light
hop notes.

Comments A rounded malt-accented beer from
DAB's great rival. The neon-lit 'U' sign above the
brewery is one of the great landmarks of Dortmund:
the union indicates the merger of a dozen small
companies a century ago. DUB's beers are *kräuse*ned
during conditioning: some partly fermented wort is
added to the lagering tanks to encourage a powerful
second fermentation. DUB's superb **Export** is now
hard to find; Dortmund brewers are turning their backs
on this style and concentrating on Pilsener for overseas
markets.

Draught version (unpasteurised) available in
Britain, Italy, Luxembourg and Spain.

Eichbaum
Eichbaum Brauereien AG, Kafertalerstrasse 170,
6800 Mannheim 1

Ureich Pils

10ABV 4%; OG 1045°

Ingredients Pale malt. Hallertau and Tettnang
hops. Bottom-fermenting yeast. Conditioned for four
weeks.

TASTING NOTES

Nose Light malt, hop and citric fruit aromas.

Palate Good balance of malt and hop in the mouth,
dry finish with delicate hop character.

Comments A well-made Pilsener beer brewed by a
company whose history dates back to 1679 in
Mannheim, though the present site has a modern,
'state of the art' high-tech brewhouse. Eichbaum
produces a wide range of beers, including a stronger
Pilsener Eichkrone, an **Export**, seasonal **Bocks**
and a smoked wheat beer, **Rauch Weissen**.

Draught version (pasteurised) available in Britain,
France and Yugoslavia.
  Bottled version (pasteurised) available in Britain,
France, Italy and Spain.

Erdinger

Privatbrauerei Erdinger Weissbräu, Werner
Brombach GmbH, Lange Zeile 1–3, W-8058
Erding

Erdinger Hefe-Weissbier

ABV 5.2%; OG 1051°

Ingredients Brauweizen wheat, pale malt.
Hallertau hops. Top-fermenting yeast. Conditioned
for two months.

TASTING NOTES

Nose Superb apple and cloves aroma.

Palate Refreshing grain and tart fruit in the mouth,
lingering bitter-sweet finish with some fruit.

Comments A classic wheat beer recalling the days
of German brewing before the arrival of modern
lagering. Erdinger is a small privately owned
brewery 50 km south-east of Munich with a vigorous
export policy. It uses a special variety of wheat
developed for brewing and grown by farmers in the
neighbourhood. Natural water comes from an
underground lake thought to be two million years
old. Traditionally, hops are used sparingly in wheat
beers and act more as a preservative than as a
bittering agent. 'Hefe-Weissbier' means wheat beer
with yeast: the finished beer is not filtered and is
therefore cloudy in the glass with a natural

Champagne sparkle. Erdinger also exports a filtered version called **Kristallklar**.

Bottled version (unpasteurised) available in Belgium, Britain, France, Greece, Italy, Luxembourg, the Netherlands, Poland, Sweden and Switzerland.

Erdinger Pinkantus

Weizenbock

ABV 7.3%; OG 1071°

Ingredients Brauweizen wheat, pale malt. Hallertau hops. Top-fermenting yeast. Conditioned for two months.

TASTING NOTES

Nose Ripe fruit and malt aromas.

Palate Tart fruit and grain in the mouth, deep bitter-sweet finish.

Comments A powerful *Bock* or strong beer, tawny coloured, with a warming, rounded appeal.

B ottled version (unpasteurised) available in Britain, France, Italy, the Netherlands, Luxembourg and Switzerland.

Hacker-Pschorr
Hacker-Pschorr Bräu GmbH,
Schwanthalerstrasse 113, 8000 Munich 2

Münchener Hell

ABV 4.9%; degrees Plato 11.4; OG 1045°

Ingredients Pale malt. Hallertau and Tettnang hops. 20 units of bitterness. Single-decoction mash. Bottom-fermenting yeast. Conditioned for one month.

TASTING NOTES

Nose Light malt aroma.

Palate Quenching bitter-sweet malt and hops in the mouth, malty finish.

Comments A rare example of an exported version of a classic Bavarian everyday beer – the German equivalent of a British 'running bitter'. *Hell* or *helles* means light or pale: it is the beer Bavarians drink in beer gardens and beer houses either with a snack or when they are out with friends for a drink or two. Hacker-Pschorr is the result of the merger of two Munich breweries, and in turn is now part of the Paulaner group but retains its own identity.

Draught version (pasteurised) available in Britain and Italy.

Edelhell Export

ABV 5.5%; degrees Plato 12.7; OG 1051°

Ingredients Pale malt. Hallertau and Tettnang hops. 24 units of bitterness. Single-decoction mash. Bottom-fermenting yeast. Conditioned for two months.

TASTING NOTES

Nose Rich malt aroma with creamy vanilla notes.

Palate Delicate refreshing malt and hop in mouth, light malt finish becoming dry.

Comments A premium Munich beer, with a generous rounded maltiness.

Draught version (pasteurised) available in Austria, Britain, Italy, Spain and Switzerland.
Bottled version (pasteurised) available in Austria, Britain, France, Greece and Switzerland.

Pschorr-Bräu Weisse

ABV 5.4%; degrees Plato 12.7; OG 1051°

Ingredients Pale barley malt and wheat malt. Hallertau hops. 17 units of bitterness. Double-decoction mash. Top-fermenting yeast. Conditioned for one month.

TASTING NOTES

Nose Pronounced cloves aroma.

Palate Tart apple fruit in the mouth, biscuity grain and aromatic fruit finish.

Comments A fine example of a Bavarian wheat beer, named after Georg
Pschorr, founder of the original brewery. The beer is unfiltered, throws a vast, fluffy head and has a both a yeasty haze and a spritzy sparkle in the glass. The beer is marketed as 'natural': wheat beers are enjoying a great revival in Germany as they are perceived as healthy and 'green'.

Draught version (pasteurised) available in Italy and Switzerland.
Bottled version (pasteurised) available in Austria, Britain, France, Italy and Switzerland.

Oktoberfest Mäzen

ABV 5.6%; degrees Plato 13.6; OG 1055°

Ingredients Pale malt. Hallertau and Tettnang hops. 20 units of bitterness. Double-decoction mash. Bottom-fermenting yeast. Conditioned for two months.

TASTING NOTES

Nose Rich malt aroma with gentle resiny hop character.

Palate Creamy grain in the mouth, deep dry finish with biscuity malt and peppery hop.

Comments The Märzen is another of the great Munich classics, traditionally brewed in March and stored for the world-famous Oktoberfest beer festival in the autumn. The style has been redefined by some brewers in recent years: the long lagering period has been reduced and the amber colour has been replaced by a more conventional pale gold but Hacker-Pschorrs has a pleasing copper tone. The company are vigorous exporters – their beers are on sale in the USA and the Far East as well as Europe – and are firmly opposed to any licensing of their brands with overseas brewers.

Draught version (pasteurised) available in Austria, France and Italy.
Bottled version (pasteurised) available in Austria, Britain and Italy.

Herford
Brauerei Felsenkeller Herford, Gebr Uekermann
GmbH & Co, 4900 Herford, Postfach 13 51

Herforder Pils

ABV 4.8%; degrees Plato 12; OG 1046°

Ingredients Premium Pilsener pale malt. 60%
bittering Hallertau Northern Brewer, 40% aroma
Perle and Tettnang hops. 32 units of bitterness.
Bottom-fermenting yeast.

TASTING NOTES

Nose Rich malt and honey aroma.

Palate Rounded grain and hop with long, dry and
delicate finish and some light citric fruit notes.

Comments An impressive example of a genuine
Pilsener beer with a superb aroma and fine hop
character.

Draught version (unpasteurised) available in Italy.
Bottled version (unpasteurised) available in
Britain and Italy.
   Herford, in Rhineland-Westphalia, also produces
an **Export**, a **Mai-Bock** and a **Doppel-Bock**.

Jever

Friesiches Bräuhaus zu Jever. Postfach 260,
D-2942 Jever. Head office: Bavaria-St Pauli-
Brauerei AG, Hopfenstrasse 15, D-2000
Hamburg 4

Jever Pils

ABV 4.9%; OG 1046°

Ingredients Pale malt from two-row barley.
Hallertau and Tettnang hops. 44 units of bitterness.
Infusion mash. Bottom-fermenting yeast.
Conditioned for 90 days.

TASTING NOTES

Nose Rich aromas of malt and hop.

Palate Delicate and refreshing balance of malt and
hop in the mouth leading into stunningly dry finish
with superb blend of hop and honey sweetness.

Comments This is Pilsener-style brewing at its
best. Spring water, a carefully cultivated yeast
strain, the finest malting barley and a generous hop
rate combine to produce a beer that is temptingly
aromatic, quenching and dramatically dry in its
finish, the dryness offset by a light sweetness.

Draught version (pasteurised) available in Britain, France, Italy, the Netherlands, Spain and USSR.

Bottled version (pasteurised) available in Britain, Finland, France, Greece, Italy, the Netherlands, Spain, Sweden, Switzerland and USSR.

As the name of the brewing group suggests, brewers in northern Germany, including the international Holsten group, were keen to emulate the new lager beers from the south in the nineteenth century. Jever is a resort town and has had its present brewery since the 1840s. Friesland was once a small independent state, a buffer between Denmark, Germany and the Netherlands, and its population traditionally enjoys exceptionally bitter drinks.

Kaltenberg

Schlossbrauerei Kaltenberg, Irmingard
Prinzessin von Bayern GmbH, Schloss-strasse 8,
8085 Geltendorf

Kaltenberg

ABV 4.9%; degrees Plato 12.5

Ingredient Pale malt. Hallertau hops. 28–30 units
of bitterness. Double-decoction mash. Bottom-
fermenting yeast. Conditioned for four to six weeks.

TASTING NOTES

Nose Fine aroma of light malt and peppery hop.

Palate Balanced hop and malt in the mouth, delicate
bitter-sweet finish.

Comments A fine Bavarian beer brewed in a fairy-
tale castle near Munich by Crown Prince Luitpold of
Kaltenberg, great-grandson of the last King Ludwig
of Bavaria (the brewery is registered in the name of
the princes wife, Princess Irmingard). Prince
Luitpold sells his beers with great élan in Germany
and abroad but is blocked from having his own tent at
the Munich Oktoberfest by the city's commercial
brewers. The prince opened a tavern with its own
micro-brewery in Munich to qualify as a brewer in
the city but the local brewers, with the connivance of
the council, then changed the rules of the beer
festival so that only companies brewing there prior to
1970 could have a festival tent.

Draught version (unpasteurised) available in
Britain and Sweden.
   Bottled version (unpasteurised) available in Austria
and Sweden.

König Ludwig Dunkel

ABV 5.6%; degrees Plato 13.3

Ingredients Pale malt and chocolate malt. Hallertau hops. 24–26 units of bitterness. Triple-decoction mash. Bottom-fermenting yeast. Conditioned for six to eight weeks.

TASTING NOTES

Nose Malt and chocolate aroma.

Palate Light, refreshing malt in the mouth, dry finish with some coffee notes.

Comments The beer is named in memory of Prince Luitpold's great-grandfather and recalls the period when the first lager beers of Bavaria were dark – *dunkel*. The style was overtaken in popularity by pale beers but there has been a renaissance in recent years, with Kaltenberg's in the van. The castle has its own beer gardens and vast quantities of the coppery *Dunkel* and a strong **Bock** are consumed there in June every year when the prince stages a medieval joust with 'knights' dressed in period costumes. He may be preparing his troops for a march on Munich.

Draught version (unpasteurised) available in Sweden.
  Bottled version (unpasteurised) available in Austria, the Netherlands and Sweden.

Prinzregent Luitpold Weissbier

ABV 5.6%; degrees Plato 12.5

Ingredients Pale malt (50%), wheat malt (50%). Hallertau hops. 14–16 units of bitterness. Double-decoction mash. Top-fermenting yeast.

TASTING NOTES

Nose Tempting apple and citrus fruit aromas.

Palate Slightly tart in the mouth, long bitter-sweet and fruity finish.

Comments The freshness of Kaltenberg's beers is enhanced by the prince's refusal to pasteurise them. This classic Bavarian wheat beer has a beautifully aromatic nose and a quenching palate.

Draught and bottled versions (unpasteurised) available in Austria and Switzerland.
British readers should note that Kaltenberg Diät Pils is brewed under licence by Whitbread.

Krombacher
Krombacher Brauerei, Bernhard Schadeberg
GmbH & Co, Hagener Strasse 261, D-5910
Kreuztal-Krombach

Krombacher Pils

ABV 4.8%; degrees Plato 11.6

Ingredients Pale malt. Hallertau and Tettnang
hops. Units of bitterness 24–26. Double-decoction
mash. Bottom-fermenting yeast. Conditioned for one
month.

TASTING NOTES

Nose Light malt aroma.

Palate Delicate balance of malt and hop in the
mouth, dry finish with good hop character.

Comments A well-made Pilsener with a malty
emphasis in the aroma and a resiny hop character in
the finish. Krombacher, in the Cologne area, believes
that an important element of the beer's character lies
in the rock spring water discovered 300 years ago.

Draught version (unpasteurised) available in
Austria, Belgium, Britain, France, Greece, Italy,
the Netherlands, Spain, Sweden and Switzerland.
Bottled version (pasteurised) available as above.

Kronen
Kronen Brauerei Dortmund GmbH & Co,
Kronenburgallee 1, 4600 Dortmund 1

Kronen Pils

ABV 5%; degrees Plato 11.4; OG 1045°

Ingredients Pale malt. Hallertau hops. 32 units of bitterness. Bottom-fermenting yeast. Conditioned for one month.

TASTING NOTES

Nose Delicate hop and grain aromas.

Palate Light and refreshing in the mouth, lingering bitter-sweet finish.

Comments A distinctive Pilsener beer from a family-owned brewery with roots that date back to the fifteenth century. *Kronen* means crown and the brewery's origins lies in an ancient wine tavern, the Krone. The companys beers are the most popular in Dortmund. It has its own yeast-cultivation centre and uses natural underground spring water. The beers have three stages of hopping with aromatic Hallertau varieties and is *kräuse*ned during the lagering stage.

Kronen Classic

ABV 5.3%; degrees Plato 12.1; OG 1046°

Ingredients Pale malt, Hallertau hops. 26 units of bitterness. Bottom- fermented yeast. Conditioned for one month.

TASTING NOTES

Nose Warm malt aroma.

Palate Rounded balance of malt and hop leading to lingering bitter-sweet finish.

Comments Classic is a malt-accented beer. It is called 'super premium' and is at the centre of the brewerys drive for overseas sales.

D raught version (unpasteurised) available in Britain, France, Italy and the Netherlands.
Bottled version (pasteurised) available as above.
Kronen also brews a **Dortmund Export** that, in common with its rivals, tends to stay in the shadows these days. Classic is the beer available in the Kronen brewery museum.

Löwenbräu
Löwenbräu AG, Nymphenburger Strasse 4, 8000
Munich 2

Löwenbräu Special Export

ABV 5.5%; degrees Plato 12.75; OG 1051°

Ingredients Pale malt from two-row spring barley.
Various Hallertau variety hops. 24 units of
bitterness. Double-decoction mash. Bottom-
fermenting yeast. Conditioned for five weeks.

TASTING NOTES

Nose Malt, cobnut and lemon aromas.

Palate Delicate refreshing palate, dry malty finish
with some hop notes.

Comments A distinctive, aromatic beer from
Munich's best-known brewery – best known abroad,
that is, for Löwenbräu at home is just one the several
large breweries in the city. Löwenbräu has entered
into licensing deals throughout the world that allow
its brands to be produced by other brewers. In
Britain, for example, its premium draught lager is
brewed by Allied Breweries and recently it has
allowed Allied to produce its bottled and, by Munich
standards, exceptionally hoppy Pils. Its flagship
export brand is now the Special Export.

Draught and bottled versions (pasteurised)
available in all European countries.

Hefe-Weissbier

ABV 5.2%; degrees Plato 12.2; OG 1049°

Ingredients Pale malt from two-row spring barley, pale wheat malt (more than 50%). Various Hallertau varieties of hops. 15 units of bitterness. Double-decoction mash. Top-fermenting yeast. Bottled version has second fermentation in bottle.

TASTING NOTES

Nose Fruity, cidery aromas.

Palate Estery and tartly refreshing with a lingering cidery finish.

Comments This is one beer that Löwenbräu will not license abroad. It is heavily promoting its wheat beer to meet the demand for such beers in Bavaria and abroad.

D raught version (unpasteurised) available in Austria and Italy.
   Bottled version (unpasteurised) available in all European countries.

Pinkus
Brauerei Pinkus Müller GmbH & Co KG,
Kreuzstrasse 4–10, 4400 Münster

Pinkus Alt

ABV 5.1%; degrees Plato 12.2

Ingredients Bioland Pilsener malt (60%) and wheat
malt (40%). Natural Hallertau hops. Single-decoction
mash. Top-fermenting yeast. Conditioned for four
months.

TASTING NOTES

Nose Rich vinous aroma.

Palate Ripe malt and slightly tart in the mouth, long
fruity and slightly acidic finish.

Comments Pinkus Müller is one of the most
fascinating breweries in Germany with an unusual
and distinctive range of beers based on the use of
organic malts and hops. In spite of the use of wheat
malt, the Alt is not a wheat beer in the true German
style and the company doesn't claim it to be. It is
very pale in colour and while it is a top-fermenting
'old' beer it nevertheless enjoys an exceptionally long
conditioning period in lagering tanks and is also
*kräusen*ed. The brewery deliberately encourages a
lactic culture in the lagering tanks that adds a slight
acidity to the finished beer. A restaurant is part of
the small brewery site where a house speciality is a
syrup made of fresh fruit that is added to the Alt to
take the edge of the beer's tart palate.

B ottled version (unpasteurised) available in
Britain and France.

Biere d'orge et d'houblon (cult. bio) / beer with organic malt and hops

naturtrüb und ungefiltert

CAT.1

Meisterlich gebraut mit Gerstenbraumalz und Hopfen aus kontrolliertem biologischem Vertragsanbau

5,2% vol. alc.

℮ 50 cl

500 ml 17 fl oz

Pinkus Special

Brauerei Pinkus Müller, Münster, Tel.: 0251 / 4 51 51

Pinkus Special

ABV 5.2%; degrees Plato 12.9

Ingredients Pilsener Bioland Gerstenbräu malt. Natural Hallertau hops. Single-decoction mash. Bottom-fermenting yeast. Conditioned for three months.

TASTING NOTES

Nose Rich malt aroma.

Palate Rounded grain in the mouth, long dry finish with good hop notes.

Comments Special is the company's flagship export beer and is sold on the basis of being truly organic: not only are the malt and hops grown without pesticides or chemical fertilisers but the brewing water is also untreated. Exceptional dryness in the finish seems to be a characteristic of beers brewed with organic malt, for this is also the case with two organic ales produced in Britain by Woodforde of Norfolk and Caledonian of Edinburgh. Pinkus Special is available in health food shops as well as the usual commercial outlets.

B ottled version (pasteurised) available in Belgium, Britain, Denmark, France, the Netherlands and Switzerland.

Pinkus Hefe Weizen

ABV 5.2%; degrees Plato 12.4

Ingredients Bioland wheat malt (60%) and Gersten barley malt (40%). Natural Hallertau hops. Single-decoction mash. Top-fermenting yeast. Conditioned for one month.

TASTING NOTES

Nose Light fruit aroma.

Palate Delicate and refreshing in the mouth, dry fruity finish.

Comments The balance of barley and wheat malt are reversed in the recipe for Müllers wheat beer compared to the Alt. Although units of bitterness are not stated, the hop level is quite low and plays up the quenching fruitiness of the beer.

B ottled version (unpasteurised) available in Belgium, Britain, France and Switzerland. The Pinkus Müller brewhouse is famous throughout the university city of Münster. The brewing side is tiny, producing just 10,000 hectolitres a year: there are four dining rooms attached. The Müller family started the business in 1816 as a bakery, brewery and chocolate factory. The brewing side prospered and Pinkus Müller is now the only brewery left in the city.

Warsteiner
Warsteiner Brauerei, Gebr Cramer GmbH & Co
KG, Wilhelmstrasse 5, Postfach 1366, 4788
Warstein

Warsteiner Premium Verum

ABV 4.8%; degrees Plato 11.7; OG 1045°

Ingredients Barley malt. Hallertau hops. Bottom-fermenting yeast. Conditioned for two months.

TASTING NOTES

Nose Light fruit and hops aromas.

Palate Rounded and well balanced in the mouth, delicate dry finish with some fruit notes.

Comments A well-made premium Pilsener from an ultra-modern brewery in an area of woods and lakes to the east of the Rhine and the Ruhr.

Draught and bottled versions (pasteurised) available in all EC countries.

IRELAND

Ireland and stout: it is almost tautologous to use the two words. The major producer of stout, Guinness, even uses the harp, the symbol of the Irish republic, on its labels. Yet the origins of stout lie across the Irish Sea in London. Until the pale ale revolution, all beers brewed in England were brown in colour but a new development in the early eighteenth century introduced a dark, even jet-black beer to inns and taverns. Working-class drinkers were great mixers of beer – even today many ask for a 'light and bitter', a mix of bottled pale ale and draught beer – and had developed a taste for a mix of pale brown, dark brown and 'stale' old ale. One innkeeper who brewed his own beer attempted to replicate this mixture with a new ale called entire butt. It became so popular with market porters that the style, dark, roasty and heavily hopped, became known as porter. The strongest, the *stoutest*, version of porter in a brewery was known as stout.

Porters and stouts became so popular that they spawned a modern commercial brewing industry in London. They were exported as far afield as the Baltic States and the American colonies and, naturally, to Ireland. Arthur Guinness bought a rundown brewery in Dublin in 1759 to brew porter and stout and established a brewing dynasty that now has breweries in dozens of countries and exports its products worldwide. It is so famous for its dry stout – a beer described by one company executive as 'a product that half the world can't spell and the other half can't pronounce' – that when it entered the lager market it had to set up a separate company called Harp. 'If Guinness brewed a lager people would expect it to be black,' they explained.

Porter has disappeared from Ireland. Guinness, along with Beamish and Murphy in Cork, concentrates on stout, though modern stout is lower in gravity than the porters of the eighteenth and nineteenth centuries. The chief characteristics of stout are the use of roasted malt and an exceptionally high hop rate. Roasted barley has been so highly kilned that it has little or no fermentable sugars left. It is used to give colour to the beer and a bitter chocolate and coffee aroma and palate. Although

 116

Guinness do not indicate it in their recipe, it is also usual to add some unmalted roasted barley as well.

For the Irish and British markets, Guinness in Dublin and London produces draught and bottled stouts with gravities of around 1040°. The bottled version in Ireland and some parts of England and Wales is naturally conditioned. The export beers vary in strength and can be as high as 1073° for the redoubtable **Foreign Extra Stout** sold primarily in tropical countries. The version described here is closer to the Irish version but has a more conventional European gravity. Both Beamish and Murphy are now owned by thrusting international corporations and their stouts are likely to be distributed more widely in the 1990s. Murphy's Stout is brewed under licence in Britain by Whitbread and therefore does not qualify for inclusion in this book.

The pale ale market in Ireland is tiny and none of it is cask-conditioned. The bitters brewed in the republic tend to be amber in colour and malt accented in the Scottish style.

Beamish
Beamish & Crawford PLC, Main Street, Cork

Beamish Stout

ABV 4.2%; degrees Plato 9.5; OG 1039°

Ingredients Pale malt, stout malt, malted wheat, roast barley, wheat syrup. Spring water. Hallertau, Irish Northdown, Perle hops and Styrian Goldings for aroma. 38–44 units of bitterness. Top-fermenting yeast.

TASTING NOTES

Nose Rich aromas of roast barley and Goldings.

Palate Roast barley, chocolate and hops in the mouth, bitter finish with some fruit and hop notes and slight astringency.

Comments Beamish stout is less assertively dry than Guinness and Murphys and has a delectably smooth, creamy appeal.

Draught and bottled versions (pasteurised) available in Britain, France and Italy.
The company dates from 1790. It was bought by Carling O'Keefe of Canada in the 1960s and both Carling and Beamish are now part of Fosters, the Australian lager group.

Guinness

Arthur Guinness & Son (Dublin) Ltd, St James's
Gate, Dublin 8

Guinness Export Stout

ABV 5.1%; degrees Plato 12; OG 1048°

Ingredients Pale malt and roast malt. Galena,
Nugget and Target hops. Units of bitterness 49.
Programmed temperature rise in mash vessel, wort
run off from lauter tun. Top-fermenting yeast.

TASTING NOTES

Nose Pronounced roast barley notes and enormous
hop character.

Palate Complex bitter-sweet balance of roast
barley, fruit and hop. Immense finish with coffee and
chocolate notes and hop bitterness.

Comments A world classic beer of enormous
complexity. It begins with splendid appeal in the
glass, the jet-black body crowned by a deep coffee-
white head. The nose is assaulted by a brilliant mix
of aromas that continues into the mouth and finish. It
is best enjoyed when drunk at a conventional ale
temperature that allows all the aromas and flavours
to develop.

Draught version (pasteurised) available in Austria, Belgium, Denmark, Finland, France, Germany, Italy, Luxembourg, the Netherlands, Spain and Switzerland.

Bottled version (pasteurised) available in Austria, Belgium, Cyprus, Denmark, Finland, France, Germany, Gibraltar, Greece, Iceland, Italy, Luxembourg, Malta, the Netherlands, Norway, Portugal, Spain, Switzerland and Turkey.

Smithwick
Irish Ale Breweries Ltd, E Smithwick & Son Ltd,
St Francis Abbey Brewery, Kilkenny

Kilkenny Ale

ABV 5.4%; degrees Plato 13; OG 1052°

Ingredients Pale ale and roasted malt. Challenger,
Fuggles, Goldings, Northdown and Northern Brewer
hops. 32.5 units of bitterness. Infusion mash. Top-
fermenting yeast.

TASTING NOTES

Nose Malt aroma with pear-drop esters.

Palate Light malty palate, dry finish with some fruit
and hop notes.

Comments The use of roast malt gives the beer a
rich copper colour and a pleasing fruity appeal.

Draught version (pasteurised) available in
Belgium, Denmark, France, Germany, Italy and
the Netherlands.

Bottled version (pasteurised) available in Belgium,
Denmark, France, Germany, Italy, the Netherlands
and Switzerland.

Smithwick, based in the country town of Kilkenny,
has been turned into 'Irish Ale Breweries', jointly
owned by Guinness and Allied Breweries of Britain.

ITALY

Italy is in the throes of a beer revolution. The country is high on the export list of other European brewers and British ales are in great demand. British-style pubs have opened in Milan and other major northern cities, and a glossy journal *La Birra del Mondo* – the World of Beer – has been an astonishing success. The reasons for this remarkable renaissance are connected to 'life style' – a belief among the young that beer is healthier than wine, which they see drunk in vast quantities by an older generation whose attitudes they challenge. There is also a powerful Austro-German influence in the region of the South Tyrol (Trentino-Alto Adige). As a result, the everyday light lagers that dominate the market are complemented by beers close in style to the bocks, double bocks, dark beers and March beers produced by Italys German-speaking neighbours.

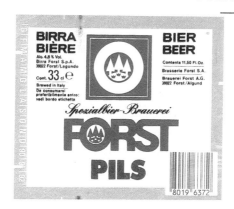

Forst
Birra Forst SPA/Brauerei Forst AG, Via val
Venosata 8, 1-39022 Lagundo
BZ/Vinschgauerstrasse 8, Postfach 29, 1-39022
Algund BZ

Forst Pils

ABV 4.8%; degrees Plato 12; OG 1047°

Ingredients Pale malt and maize. Hallertau hops.
Units of bitterness 28–32. Double-decoction mash.
Bottom-fermenting yeast. Conditioned for two
months.

TASTING NOTES

Nose Light malt aroma.

Palate Rounded balance of malt and hop in the
mouth, dry malt and vanilla finish.

Comments As the bilingual name and address
indicates, Forst is in the South Tyrol, close to the
Austrian border. The pilsener is well-rounded and
malty in the Munich tradition. Forst also produces a
4.4% **Premium** a 5% **Kronen** and 6.5% **Sixtus** that
is brewed from chocolate, crystal and dark malts.

Draught version (unpasteurised) available in
Austria.
   Bottled version (pasteurised) available in Austria,
Britain and Yugoslavia.

Moretti
Birra Moretti SPA, Viale Venezia 9, 33100 Udine

Birra Friulana

ABV 4.5%; degrees Plato 11.3

Ingredients Pale malt and maize (30%). Hallertau
hops. 21 units of bitterness. Double-decoction mash.
Bottom-fermenting yeast. Conditioned for one
month.

TASTING NOTES

Nose Mellow malt aroma with delicate hop resin
notes.

Palate Clean and quenching; dry finish,
predominantly malty with hints of honey and vanilla.

Comments Refreshing lightly hopped beer.

La Rossa

ABV 7.5%; degrees Plato 19.3

Ingredients Pale malt (10%), dark malt (90%).
Hallertau and Spalt hops. 24 units of bitterness.
Double-decoction mash. Bottom-fermenting yeast.
Conditioned for two months.

TASTING NOTES

Nose Rich malt aroma.

Palate Deep malt and hop in the mouth, peppery
hop finish with malt and some fruit.

Comments A copper-coloured beer with a profound
malt character and good spicy hop, similar to a
Munich March beer.

B ottled version (pasteurised) available in Austria,
Britain, Germany, Greece, the Netherlands and
Yugoslavia.

Moretti, founded in Udine to the north of Venice,
was family owned until it became a member of the
Canadian Labatt group. The company began
brewing in 1859 when the region of Friuli was still
annexed to the Austro-Hungarian empire, an
association that lingers on in the style of the La Rossa
beer. Moretti moved to a custom-built new brewery
in 1984 and now produces 450,000 hectolitres a year.

The company's famous trademark of the man with
the moustache is based on a regular drinker of
Moretti's beer who was spotted supping one day at a
taverna by a sharp-eyed marketing man. In the
drinker's honour, Moretti brews a special beer called
Baffo d'Oro – Golden Moustache.

Peroni
Birra Peroni Industriale SPA, G A Guattini 6/A,
00161 Rome

Nastro Azzuro

ABV 5.3%; degrees Plato 12.5; OG 1050°

Ingredients Alexis and Prisma pale malts, 20
maize. Saaz hops. Bottom-fermenting yeast.
Conditioned for ten weeks.

TASTING NOTES

Nose Malt and light citric fruit aromas.

Palate Refreshing in the mouth, bitter-sweet finish
with light hop notes.

Comments Nastro Azzuro – Blue Riband – is the
main beer produced by Italy's biggest brewing
group.

D raught version (pasteurised) available in France.
Bottled version (pasteurised) available in
Austria, Britain, France, Germany, Greece, the
Netherlands and Switzerland.

L U X E M B O U R G

The Grand Duchy of Luxembourg has five breweries
to meet the demands of a population of 350,000
famed for its zeal for good eating and drinking. The
tiny duchy is surrounded by Germany, France and
the Belgian region also known as Luxembourg.
Germany has made the greatest impact on beer
styles in the duchy, where the emphasis is on lager
beers generally of the Pilsener variety, though they
tend to be malty and less hoppy than the beers across
the German border and are not brewed according to
the *Reinheitsgebot*. For the home market the
Luxembourg brewers produce a few Bocks and
seasonal specials.

Bofferding
Brasserie Nationale SA, 2 Boulevard John F
Kennedy, L-4930 Bascharage

Bofferding

ABV 4.8%; degrees Plato 11.8

Ingredients Pale malt and corn. Hallertau
Northern Brewer and aroma hops. Units of bitterness
25. Infusion mash. Bottom-fermenting yeast.
Conditioned for one month.

TASTING NOTES

Nose Delicate aromas of malt and hop resin.

Palate Refreshing balance of malt and hops with
light bitter-sweet finish.

Comments A pleasant aromatic light lager with a
good hop character.

Draught and bottled versions (unpasteurised)
available in Belgium.

Mousel and Clausen

Brasserie Reunies de Luxembourg Mousel et Clausen SA, BP 371, L-2013 Luxembourg-Clausen

Mousel Premium Pils

ABV 4.8%; degrees Plato 11.4; OG 1047°

Ingredients Selected pale malts from two-row spring barley (90%), rice (10%). Hallertau and Saaz hops. 28.5 units of bitterness. Double-decoction. Bottom-fermenting yeast. Conditioned for five weeks.

TASTING NOTES

Nose Rich malt aroma with hop notes developing.

Palate Delicate malt and hop in the mouth, light hoppy finish.

Comments A well-crafted and well-conditioned Pilsener from an aggressively growing company that acquired the Henri Funck brands in 1982. Mousel and Clausen also exports **Henri Funck Strong Lager**: it has exactly the same specification as Mousel Premium Pils but is less assertively hoppy.

Draught version (pasteurised) available in Belgium, Britain, France and Germany.
Bottled version (pasteurised) available in Belgium, Britain, France, Germany, Romania and Spain.

THE NETHERLANDS

The Netherlands has close geographic and linguistic links with Belgium yet the beer scene is dramatically different. Compared to its Low Countries neighbour, the Netherlands has only a handful of breweries and the beer market is distorted by the awesome power and dominance of Heineken. Grolsch may be the second biggest brewer in the country but it is tiny by comparison, even though it has achieved cult international status. The small brewers in the Netherlands are so busy producing beer for their own market, in order to satisfy drinkers looking for an alternative to Heineken and its stablemate Amstel, that they have little opportunity to engage in exporting.

From Heineken down, the Netherlands beer market is dominated by lager beers in the Pilsener style but there is welcome variety in the form of brown beers, known as *Oud Bruin* – Old Brown, seasonal Bocks, a few wheat beers and some Munich-style dark lagers. Choice has been improved by the appearance of a few micro-brewers in recent years. The country has one monastic brewery, Schaapskooi – sheepfold – in Tilburg, near the Belgian border. As well as its own top-fermenting ales, it provides abbey beers to the nearby Breda brewery, owned by the British Allied Breweries group, which markets them within the Netherlands.

More than any other European country, the Netherlands requires a visit from the dedicated beer lover if the countrys products are to be appreciated to the full and if the belief that it produces only Pilsener lagers is to be dispelled. The splendid Gulpen brewery in the Limburg region, for example, brews a top-fermenting Altbier that has a strong following in Belgium. It is a blend of beers, one of which has been allowed to ferment with wild yeasts. The end result is a slightly sour, dark and refreshing beer. Also in Limburg, De Ridder, now owned by Heineken, has a Bock and the intriguingly named dark, Maltezer, with a colour and soft sweetness derived from caramel. Gulpener Aajt now has limited distribution outside the Netherlands and it is to be hoped that other fascinating contributions to the beer world will find a wider audience in the years ahead.

Alfa
Alfa Bierbrowerij, Thull 15–19, 6365 AC
Schinnen

Alfa Beer

ABV 5%; degrees Plato 12; OG 1048°

Ingredients Pale and Munich malt from France and the Netherlands. Hallertau, Saaz and Tettnang hops. 19 units of bitterness. Double-decoction mash. Bottom-fermenting yeast. Conditioned for two months.

TASTING NOTES

Nose Good balance of malt and hop aromas.

Palate Smooth and rounded in the mouth, delicate hop finish.

Comments A clean-tasting, well-made lager from a small brewery with a staff of 30 in the Limburg region sandwiched between Belgium and Germany. Alfa is family-owned and takes great pride in the use of local spring water, all-malt recipes and, by modern standards, a long lagering period.

Bottled version (pasteurised) available in Britain and Italy.

Alfa is also brews a **Super-Dort** in the Dortmund style, 7% ABV, malty and sweet.

Arcen
De Arcense Bierbrouwerij BV, Kruisweg 44,
5944 EN Arcen

Arcener Stoom Bier

ABV 5%; degrees Plato 12

Ingredients Pale malt and wheat malt. Hallertau
Northern Brewer bittering hops, Hersbrücker Spät
aroma hops. 22 units of bitterness. Top-fermenting
yeast.

TASTING NOTES

Nose Delicate fruit aromas with good peppery hop
notes.

Palate Refreshing light fruit, dry finish with good
hop character.

Comments The balance between barley and wheat
malt is not disclosed but the beer has a fine
quenching and lightly fruity character.

B ottled version (pasteurised) available in Belgium,
France, Italy and Spain.

Arcener Tarwe

ABV 5%; degrees Plato 11.5

Ingredients Pale malt (50%) and wheat malt (50%). Hallertau Northern Brewer and Hersbrücker Spät hops. 17 units of bitterness. Top-fermenting yeast a Bavarian wheat beer culture.

TASTING NOTES

Nose Cidery apple fruit aroma.

Palate Rich and refreshing light fruit drying into bitter-sweet finish.

Comments A careful and well-made recreation of a classic Bavarian wheat beer, with a yeast culture brought from Germany. Lightly hopped, the beer develops a fine fruity aroma and palate. It has a second fermentation in the bottle and meets the requirements of the German *Reinheitsgebot*.

B ottled version (unpasteurised) available in Belgium, France, Italy and Spain.

Arcener Stout

ABV 6.5%; degrees Plato 16.5

Ingredients Pale, chocolate, Munich and coloured malts plus caramel. Hallertau Northern Brewer and Hersbrücker Spät hops. 27 units of bitterness. Top-fermenting yeast.

TASTING NOTES

Nose Rich malt and chocolate notes.

Palate Coffee and chocolate in the mouth, dry and bitter finish.

Comments A pleasingly rounded stout dominated by the dark malts.

Bottled version (pasteurised) available in Belgium, France, Italy and Spain.

Arcener is a small but modern brewery in the Limburg region with an impressive range of top-fermenting beers that includes **Bocks** and an **Altbier**. It also produces a separate range of ales under the Hertog Jan label.

Brand
Koninklijke Brand Bierbrouwerij BV, Postbus 1,
6300 AA Wijlre

Brand Pils

ABV 5%; degrees Plato 11.8–11.9; OG 1048°

Ingredients West European pale malt from 2-row
summer barley (90%), maize grits (10%). Hallertau
Northern Brewer, Perle and Hersbrücker hops.
26–28 units of bitterness. Mix of infusion and
decoction mashing. Bottom-fermenting yeast.
Conditioned for 42 days.

TASTING NOTES

Nose Light malt and hop aroma.
boPalatebf Delicate malt in the mouth, light dry
finish with some hop notes.

Comments A light and refreshing Pilsener sold in a
white ceramic-style bottle. Marketed as 'Royal
Brand Beer' in North America.

Draught version (unpasteurised) available in
Belgium and Germany.
Bottled version (unpasteurised) available in
Belgium, France and Italy.

Brand Up

ABV 5.5%; degrees Plato 12.4; OG 1050°

Ingredients 100 West European pale malt from 2-row summer barley. Hersbrücker, Spalt and Tettnang hops. 36–38 units of bitterness. Mix of infusion and decoction mashing. Bottom-fermenting yeast. Conditioned for 4956 days.

TASTING NOTES

Nose Strong hop and citric fruit aroma.

Palate Fine balance of malt and hop, lingering hop and lemon finish.

Comments Not to be confused with Seven Up – the Up is short for *Urtyp* – Brand Up is a superb hoppy beer: 'one of the best Pilseners in Europe!' says the head brewer, no slouch at blowing his own trumpet. It is brewed in the true German all-malt tradition, with a long lagering period to produce a complex and delicate aroma and palate.

D raught and bottled versions (unpasteurised) available in Belgium and Germany.

Brand Imperator

ABV 6.5–7%; degrees Plato 17.4; OG 1072°

Ingredients 100 pale, chocolate and Münich malts. Hallertau, Hersbrücker and Perle hops. 21–22 units of bitterness. Mix of infusion and decoction mashing. Bottom-fermenting yeast. Conditioned for 49–56 days.

TASTING NOTES

Nose Rich malt aroma with a touch of vanilla.

Palate Creamy and slightly sweet with delicate hop finish.

Comments An amber Bock beer with a rounded malt character.

Draught and bottled versions (unpasteurised) available in Belgium.

The brewery is the oldest in the Netherlands and dates from 1871 though there has been a brewery in the small town of Wyrle since the fourteenth century. The company supplies the Dutch royal family, hence the Royal Dutch tag in some export markets. Brand prides itself on the high quality of the ingredients it uses, the long lagering period and its refusal to pasteurise its beers. Its comment that 'there is no need to pasteurise – pasteurisation serves to lengthen the shelf-life of a beer but only marginally and at enormous costs to the taste and aroma of the beer' should be hung in every brewer's office throughout the world.

Grolsch
Grolsche Bierbrouwerij, Fazantstraat 2, 7523 EA
Enschede

Grolsch Premium Lager

ABV 5%; OG 1047°

Ingredients Pilsener malt from spring barley from
Belgium, England, France, Germany and the
Netherlands. Small percentage of maize. Hallertau
and Saaz hops, aroma hops added at end of copper
boil. 27 units of bitterness. Double-decoction mash.
Bottom-fermenting yeast. Conditioned for ten weeks.

TASTING NOTES

Nose Floral hop and delicate fresh-mown grass
aromas.

Palate Some citric fruit notes in the mouth, gentle
bitter-sweet finish with good hop character.

Comments The success of Grolsch should not be
allowed to detract from its quality. In an age when
too many lager beers masquerade as Pilseners, are
conditioned for not much longer than ales and then
have any taste destroyed by clumsy pasteurisation,
the brewery based in Enschede and Groenlo near the
German border has refused to pander to the worst
aspects of mass marketing. Its Premium Lager –
called Pilsener in the Netherlands – has a long, slow
conditioning that produces a beautifully balanced

beer that in its bottled form is not pasteurised even for export, which in Grolschs case includes some 40 countries. Its 'swing-top' bottle with the ceramic stopper has become a cult and other brewers have hurried to copy it.

D raught version (pasteurised) available in Britain. Bottled version (unpasteurised) available in Britain, France, Germany, Italy, Portugal, Spain and Sweden.

For the home market Grolsch also brews a top-fermenting **Amber** with 20–30% wheat, a **Bock** and an **Oud Bruin**.

Gulpener
BV Gulpener Bierbrouwerij, Rijksweg 16, 6271
AE Gulpen

Gulpener Dort

ABV 6.5%; degrees Plato 16;OG 1065°

Ingredients Pale malt, maize and caramel.
Hallertau hops. 20 units of bitterness. Double-
decoction mash. Bottom-fermenting yeast.
Conditioned for ten weeks.

TASTING NOTES

Nose Rich malt aroma.

Palate Sweet malt in the mouth, soft finish with
some hop notes.

Comments An aromatic, well-rounded beer that
benefits from long conditioning and lack of
pasteurisation.

Draught and bottled versions (unpasteurised)
available in France.

Mestreechs Aajt

ABV 3.5%; degrees Plato 8.5; OG 1034°

Ingredients Pale malt and sugar. Hallertau hops. 10 units of bitterness. Double-decoction mash. Spontaneous fermentation. Conditioned for at least one year.

TASTING NOTES

Nose Hints of sourness and cherry fruit

Palate Gentle sour fruit in the mouth. Dry, bitter-sweet finish.

Comments A brown beer in a cradled and cork-stoppered bottle. Brewed in the Belgian tradition, using wild yeasts for fermentation, it is a rich-tasting and deeply refreshing beer.

B ottled version (unpasteurised) available in Britain.

Gulpen is based near Maastricht in the well-breweried Limburg region. It is a small craft brewery founded in 1825 and has a high reputation in its home country for its range of beers, which includes a **Pils**, the premium **X-pert**, an **Oud Bruin** and a **Bock** as well as the sour, Belgian-style **Alt**. The company also sells vinegar and mustard.

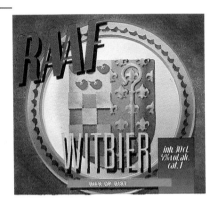

Raaf
Brouwerij Museum Raaf, Rijksweg 232, 6582 AB
Heumen

Witbier

ABV 5%; degrees Plato 12.5

Ingredients Pilsener malt and wheat malt.
Hersbrcker and Perle hops. Top-fermenting yeast.

TASTING NOTES

Nose Orange fruit aroma.

Palate Light citric fruit in the mouth, bitter-sweet
fruity finish.

Comments A well-made and quenching wheat beer
produced in a brewery attached to a brewery
museum. Tel: (080) 581177 for information.

Tripel

ABV 8.5%; degrees Plato 19.6

Ingredients Pilsener malt. Hersbrücker and Perle hops. Top-fermenting yeast.

TASTING NOTES

Nose Rich and aromatic fruit and hop.

Palate Refreshing balance of malt, fruit and hop with a slightly vinous finish.

Comments A powerful beer with some slight lactic sourness.

Draught version (unpasteurised) available in Belgium.
  Bottled version (unpasteurised) available in France.

St-Christoffel

Bierbrouwerij St-Christoffel, Bredeweg 14, 6042
GG Roermond

Christoffel Bier

ABV 5.1%; degrees Plato 11.9

Ingredients 100 malt. Hallertau and Hersbrücker
hops. 45 units of bitterness. Infusion mash.
Conditioned for two months.

TASTING NOTES

Nose Massive resiny hop aroma.

Palate Hoppy on the tongue, long dry and bitter
finish.

Comments Not a beer for softies – one of the
hoppiest and driest beers in the world. Directors of
vast international brewing combines who are foisting
on the world 'light' and 'dry' beers that are devoid of
taste and character should be locked in a room and
forced to drink Christoffel for a day or two!

D raught version (unpasteurised) available in
Belgium.
   The brewery was founded by Leo Brand of the
Brand brewing family, who fancied brewing his own
thing and named the brewery after the patron
saint of Roermond. Mr Brand lives in the brewery
and among his equipment is a fine domed copper that
he found in a barn.

SCOTLAND

Scotland shares with England a brewing tradition
based on top-fermenting ales but there is a sharp
difference in the style brewed north of the border.
The style has been submerged for many years as a
result of the near monopolisation of the country by
two brewing giants, Bass's Tennent Caledonian and
Scottish & Newcastle, both of which have pandered
to the Scots' liking for thin lager, the ideal 'chaser'
for whisky. However, a clutch of small brewers are
now reviving the Scottish ale style.

With the exception of a sturdy micro-brewery on
Orkney and a brew-pub north of Aberdeen, Scots
brewers congregate in the lowlands and the central
belt of the country. There are good historic reasons
for this. The best malting barley for brewing is
grown in the south: the Highland varieties are better
for distilling. Before the age of modern transport,
brewers naturally settled in the area where the good
barley grew. The abundance of barley but the lack of
an indigenous hop industry created ales that were
strongly malt-accented, with imported hops used
sparingly. Pale malt is the basic ingredient of
Scottish ale but the tradition is to use generous
amounts of crystal, roast, chocolate and black malt,
too, leading to beers with a generous bitter-sweet
roasted and chocolate character.

The Scots, unlike the English and the Welsh, do
not speak about mild and bitter. Mild, whether dark
or pale, is called Light while the equivalent to bitter
is known as Heavy. Export is a definite style, a
strong premium bitter or Heavy created in the
eighteenth and nineteenth centuries when the likes of
McEwan and Younger were vigorous exporters of
their distinctive beers to the Americas, Europe and
the British colonies. Scotch Ale, a strong bottled
beer, is popular in Belgium and other countries.
Gordon's Highland Ale and the powerful Traquair
are superb examples of strong export beers and the
success of the new breed of micro-brewers in
Scotland should soon add to the list.

**THE BELHAVEN BREWERY
COMPANY LIMITED**

Belhaven
Belhaven Brewery Co Ltd, Spot Road, Dunbar,
East Lothian EH42 1RS

Belhaven Scottish Ale

ABV 3.9%; degrees Plato 10.23; OG 1041°

Ingredients Pale, crystal and black malts and
brewing sugar. British Columbian Bramlings Cross,
English Fuggles, Goldings and Whitbread Goldings
Variety hops. 28 units of bitterness. Top-fermenting
yeast.

TASTING NOTES

Nose Malt and creamy toffee aromas.

Palate Fruit and malt in the mouth, bitter-sweet
finish with vanilla notes.

Comments A smooth, creamy, easy-drinking
copper-coloured beer.

B ottled version (pasteurised) available in France
and Italy.

Belhaven Scottish Ale

ABV 4.5%; degrees Plato 11; OG 1044°

Ingredients Pale, crystal and black malts and brewing sugar. British Columbian Bramlings Cross, English Fuggles, Goldings and Whitbread Goldings Variety hops. 28 units of bitterness. Top-fermenting yeast.

TASTING NOTES

Nose Rich fruit, malt and toffee aromas.

Palate Light fruit and hop in the mouth, deep complex finish with malt, some fruit and developing hop bitterness.

Comments Delicious stronger version of the first beer with a more complex aroma and taste and greater hop appeal.

B ottled version (pasteurised) available in Italy. Belhaven, close to the English border, has handsome old buildings, with cowled maltings and ivy-covered walls. It dates back to 1719 and produces some renowned cask-conditioned beers, from a light to a strong ale, all with rich fruity aromas and palates. The brewery, part of the Control Securities group with a growing number of pubs throughout Britain, is independent of the large Scottish brewers.

Scottish & Newcastle

Scottish & Newcastle Beer Production Ltd,
Fountain Brewery, Fountain Bridge, Edinburgh,
Lothian EH3 9YY

Gordons Highland Ale

ABV 8.5%; degrees Plato 22; OG 1090°

Ingredients Pale malt, roasted barley and cereal adjunct. Fuggles, Target and Yeoman hops. 43 units of bitterness. Top-fermenting yeast.

TASTING NOTES

Nose Complex aromas of roast barley, toast and bitter chocolate.

Palate Bitter-sweet in the mouth, deep dry finish with great roast, hop and coffee notes.

Comments A beer of enormous complexity, dark in colour and with a creamy head, its characteristics result from the use of roasted barley. It is bitter and yet refreshing. Visitors to the Scottish & Newcastle sample cellar have appealed without success for the beer to be made available in Britain.

B ottled version (pasteurised) available in Belgium.

McEwans Export

ABV 4.6%; degrees Plato 10; OG 1046°

Ingredients Pale malt, roasted barley and cereal adjunct. Fuggles, Target and Yeoman hops. 24 units of bitterness. Top-fermenting yeast.

TASTING NOTES

Nose Roast and toffee aromas.

Palate Light, creamy malt in the mouth, light finish with some vanilla notes.

Comments The best-known example of a Scottish export ale. The cereal adjunct used by Scottish & Newcastle is thought to be maize.

Draught version (pasteurised) available in Italy. Bottled version (pasteurised) available in Finland.

The group is one of the biggest brewery companies in Britain, based as its name suggests in Scotland and the North-east but with pubs and free- trade agreements nationwide.

Traquair
Traquair House Brewery, Traquair House,
Innerleithen, Peeblesshire EH446PW

Traquair House Ale

ABV 7%; OG 1075°

Ingredients Pale ale and roast malt. Goldings and
Red Sell hops. Top-fermenting yeast.

TASTING NOTES

Nose Rich aromas of malt, hop, dark chocolate, rich
fruit and spices.

Palate Winey, grainy and hop resin in the mouth,
intense bitter finish with hints of pineapple and
chocolate.

Comments A dark, strong and heady brew with a
port-wine character. It is brewed in a magnificent
restored medieval house, the oldest inhabited
building in Scotland, visited by Mary Queen of Scots
and Prince Charles Edward Stuart (Bonnie Prince
Charlie). The owners of the house, the Maxwell
Stuarts, are members of the Stuart clan and keep the
main Bear Gates closed until a Stuart returns to the
British throne.

B ottled form (pasteurised) available in Belgium. The ancient brewhouse was painstakingly restored by the late 'laird' (lord of the manor). The beers – there is a 5% ABV draught **Bear Ale** as well – are the only British ones to be brewed in uncoated wooden vessels. A draught version of Traquair Ale is sold in Britain in the winter. The bottled version is popular in such far-flung and unlikely countries as Japan and the USA. The house and brewery are now run by the laird's daughter, Catherine Maxwell Stuart, and are open to visitors (Tel: 0896 830 323).

SPAIN

Spain is enjoying a beer revival in common with the other Latin countries. It has a considerable beer heritage, dating back many centuries. During the Roman empire, Pliny recorded that 'The nations of the west have their own intoxicant from grain soaked in water; there are many ways of making it in Gaul and Spain and under different names, though the principle is the same. The Spanish have taught us that these liquors keep well'. A flourishing brewing industry developed in the sixteenth century under the rule of the Emperor Charles V, who was born in Ghent and was imbued with the beer culture of the Low Countries.

The style today is certainly not Belgian. Light 'international' lagers predominate though stronger lagers are not dissimilar to a Dortmund, with a rounded malt appeal. A few companies produce dark Munich-style beers. The industry is dominated by large groups under international control. The biggest brewing concern, El Aguila, is part of Heineken while Carlsberg from Denmark, Henninger from Germany, and Kronenbourg from France have interests. The Anglo-Irish Guinness bought Cruz del Campo in late 1990 and the beers of this group may soon make their mark on the European scene. San Miguel, despite its impressively Hispanic name, originates from the Philippines.

Aguila

SA El Aguila, Fabricas de Cerveza y Malta, Vara
de Rey 7, 28045 Madrid

Aguila Pilsener

ABV 4.5%; degrees Plato 11.2; OG 1045°

Ingredients Pale malt and corn grits. Northern
Brewer and Brewers Gold hops (Spanish varieties).
23 units of bitterness. Double-decoction mash.
Bottom-fermenting yeast. Conditioned for three
weeks.

TASTING NOTES

Nose Light malt and citric fruit aromas.

Palate Bitter-sweet in the mouth. malty finish
becoming dry.

Comments Pleasant and refreshing beer that lacks
hop character.

B ottled version (pasteurised) available in Britain
and France.

Adlerbräu

ABV 5.5%; degrees Plato 13.2; OG 1053°

Ingredients Pale and caramel malt, corn grits.
Northern Brewer and Brewers Gold hops. 28 units of
bitterness. Double-decoction mash. Bottom-
fermenting yeast. Conditioned for three weeks.

TASTING NOTES

Nose Estery, fruity aromas.

Palate Quenching malt in the mouth, clean bitter-
sweet finish with light hop notes.

Comments A copper-coloured beer with a
pronounced estery aroma and refreshing appeal.

B ottled version (pasteurised) available in France.

Aguila Reserva Extra

ABV 6.5%; degrees Plato 15.2; OG 1062°

Ingredients Pale and roasted malts, corn grits.
Northern Brewer and Brewers Gold hops. 28 units of
bitterness. Double-decoction mash. Bottom-
fermenting yeast. Conditioned for three weeks.

TASTING NOTES

Nose Fragrant malt and hop aromas.

Palate Good balance in the mouth, refreshing and
delicate bitter-sweet finish.

Comments A good example of a well-rounded
'Extra', a popular style of premium lager in Spain.

Bottled version (pasteurised) available in France.
El Aguila was founded in 1900 and today brews
4,850,000 hectolitres a year. It has breweries in San
Sebastin de los Reyes, Valencia, Córdoba and
Zaragoza.

San Miguel
San Miguel Fabricas de Cerveza y Malta SA,
Carbonero y Sol 1–1a, 28006 Madrid

San Miguel Premium Lager

ABV 5.4%; degrees Plato 13

Ingredients Pale malt. Hallertau Northern Brewer
and Perle, Styrian Goldings hops. 23–25 units of
bitterness. Infusion mash. Bottom- fermenting yeast.
Conditioned for one month.

TASTING NOTES

Nose Malty, estery aromas with hop notes
developing.

Palate Smooth and malty in the mouth, bitter-sweet
with light hop character.

Comments A distinctive and malt-accented beer
balanced by some Goldings hop character.

Draught version (pasteurised) available in Britain,
France, Gibraltar, Italy, Madeira and Portugal.
   Bottled version (pasteurised) available in Belgium,
Britain, Denmark, Finland, France, Gibraltar,
Greece, Italy, Malta, the Netherlands, Portugal,
Sweden and Switzerland.

Selecta XV

ABV 5.4%; degrees Plato 13

Ingredients Pale malt. Hallertau Northern Brewer and Perle, Styrian Goldings hops. 23–25 units of bitterness. Infusion mash. Bottom-fermenting yeast. Conditioned for one month.

TASTING NOTES

Nose Fruit esters and hop aromas.

Palate Rich malt and hops in the mouth, long bitter-sweet finish.

Comments A ripe tasting, fruity and rounded premium beer.

Bottled version (pasteurised) available in Britain, France, Gibraltar and Italy.
  San Miguel began as a brewing company in the Philippines – and is still the dominant brewer there – before establishing itself in Spain. It brews some 3,800,000 hectolitres a year from breweries in Burgos, Lérida and Málaga.

SWITZERLAND

It is the German-speaking part of Switzerland that
has the strongest beer heritage, which dates back to
a monastic brewhouse in the abbey of St Gallen in the
ninth century. Four large companies dominate the
Swiss market and produce a broad range of beers,
from lagers – the Swiss are punctilious in not using
the term Pilsener unless a beer broadly matches the
Czech version – Bocks, March beers, wheat beers
and even an *Altbier*. Exporting is left to the biggest of
the groups, Hürlimann, as most effort goes into
satisfying the domestic market. A few micro-brewers
and brew-pubs have sprung up in recent years.

Hürlimann
Brauerei Hürlimann AG, PO Box 654, 8027
Zürich

Löwenbräu Lager

ABV 4.8%; degrees Plato 11.3; OG 1045°

Ingredients Pale malt. Hallertau and Hersbrücker
hops. 21 units of bitterness. Bottom-fermenting
yeast. Conditioned for two months.

TASTING NOTES

Nose Fresh aromas of malt and delicate hop resins.

Palate Refreshing in the mouth, dry, malty finish.

Comments A mild, dry lager brewed in a
subsidiary Zürich brewery to the main Hürlimann
plant. The beer has no connection with its Munich
namesake.

Draught version (pasteurised) available in Italy.
Bottled version (pasteurised) available in Britain,
France, Italy and Spain.

Sternbräu

ABV 5.5%; degrees Plato 12.6; OG 1057°

Ingredients Pale malt. Hallertau and Saaz hops. 28 units of bitterness. Bottom-fermenting yeast. Conditioned for three months.

TASTING NOTES

Nose Pronounced hoppy nose with good Saaz character.

Palate Good balance of malt and hops in the mouth, dry bitter finish.

Comments A fine-tasting lager that has enjoyed a long conditioning – a hallmark of Swiss brewing. It comes from the main Hürlimann brewery, dating from 1836 on a site that was formerly a vineyard. Although Swiss brewers are not bound to do so, Hürlimann adheres to the German Purity Pledge.

D raught version (pasteurised) available in Italy. Bottled version (pasteurised) available in Britain, Italy and Spain.

Samichlaus

ABV 14%; degrees Plato 28.5; OG 1122°

Ingredients Pale and dark malt. Hallertau, Hersbrucker and Styrian hops. 30 units of bitterness. Bottom-fermenting yeast. Conditioned for ten months.

TASTING NOTES

Nose Great depth of aromas with port wine, dried fruit, malt and peppery hop.

Palate Coffee, bitter chocolate, nuts and malt in the mouth. Bitter finish developing a Rémy Martin Cognac note.

Comments Samichlaus – Santa Claus – is officially the strongest beer in the world, registered in the Guinness Book of Records to the chagrin of the Germany EKU, which formerly held the record. Samichlaus lacks the tacky, sticky, syrupy taste of the 'headbanger' strong lagers produced for the British market. This is achieved by the long lagering period that produces a dark brown beer with a lively carbonation and a smooth if complex aroma and palate. It is brewed just once a year on December 6, when the Swiss celebrate St Nicholas, and is not released until the following December 6. Hürlimann pioneered yeast-culturing in Switzerland and uses a special strain for this remarkable beer.

Bottled version (pasteurised) available in all EC countries.
British readers should note that draught Hürlimann lagers are brewed under licence by Shepherd Neame of Faversham, Kent.

USSR

Contrary to popular opinion, alcohol and vodka are not synonymous in the Soviet Union. As a result of the size of the federation, it is one of the world's major producers of beer, though consumption places it lower down the pecking order. There are between 300 and 400 breweries, all state-owned. The major one is Zhiguli, which has several breweries strategically placed, like printing plants for Pravda, throughout the USSR and established with considerable help from the Czechs. The beer exported to the west comes from Kiev.

Zhiguli
Kiev Obolon Brewery, Bogatyrskaya Street 3,
Kiev 212

Zhiguli

ABV 4.4%; degrees Plato 11; OG 1044°

Ingredients Pale malt, brewing sugar and rice (less than 5%). Klon hops. Units of bitterness 17. Single-decoction mash. Bottom-fermenting yeast. Conditioned for 45 days.

TASTING NOTES

Nose Light malt-accented aroma.

Palate Refreshing malt in the mouth, light finish with some hop notes.

Comments A well-conditioned, quenching lager.

B ottled version (pasteurised) available in Britain.

UK importers, wholesalers, distributors and specialist beer shops dealing with imported beers

Adnams & Co, Sole Bay Brewery, Southwold, Suffolk IP18 6JW.

Ale Cellar, 114 Rosemont Viaduct, Aberdeen AB1 1NY, Grampian, Scotland.

Ale House, 79 Raglan Road, Leeds, W. Yorks.

J A Bagley, 4 Meredith Street, Manchester M14 6ST.

BB (Budweiser Budvar) Supply Centre, 91 Whitechapel High Street, London E1 7RA.

Beer from Belgium, Sale, Cheshire M33 1EH.

Beer Cellar, Bedford Road, Petersfield, Hampshire GU32 3QB.

Beer Shop, 8 Pitfield Street, London N1 6HA.

Beers of the World, Unit 19, The Tanneries, Brockhampton Lane, Havant, Hants.

Betamore Fine Food, Gravel Lane, Chigwell, Essex IG7 6DQ.

Bitter Experience, 429 Lee Road, Blackheath, London SE3.

H P Bulmer Ltd, Plough Lane, Hereford HR4 0LE.

Carlsberg Ltd, Bridge Street, Northampton NN1 1PZ.

Cave Direct, 40 Parkview Road, Welling, Kent (Belgian specialist).

Continental Beer Importers, Tresillian Terrace, Curran Road, Cardiff CF1 5DE.

Continental Lager Distributors Ltd, Ashworth Estate, 42 Beddington Lane, Croydon, Surrey CR0 4TB.

Cooks Delight, 360–364 High Street, Berkhamsted, Herts HP4 1HU (Belgian specialist).

J A Cooper Ltd, 55 Surrey Street, Glossop, Derbyshire SK13 9AJ.

Deinhard & Co Ltd, 95 Southwark Street, London SE1 0JF.

East-West Ales, Unit 1–2, Alvans Farm, Romford Road, Pembury, Kent.

Euroimpex UK Ltd, Little Hatfield, Hull 1UZ.

Fine Beers of Europe, 3 Marty's Yard, Hampstead, London NW3 1QN.

German Lager Importers Ltd, Kobi House, Alpine Way, London Industrial Park, Beckton, London E6 4LA.

Grog Blossom: branches at 66 Notting Hill Gate, London W11; 253 West End Lane, West Hampstead, London NW6.

Inter-Ale, Mason's Arms, Strawberry Bank, Cartmel Fell, Cumbria (Belgian specialist).

Jester Off-licence, 129 Castlehaven Road, Kentish Town, London NW1.

Kaltenberg UK, PO Box 7, Monson Avenue, Cheltenham, Glos.

Legendary Yorkshire Heroes, Unit 1, Off Quay Building, Foundry Lane, Ouseburn, Newcastle upon Tyne, Tyne & Wear NE6 1LH.

Löwenbräu UK, The Brewery, High Street, Romford, Essex RM1 1LA.

Maison Caurette Ltd, 144–152 Bermondsey Street, London SE1 3TQ.

C H Marlow Ltd, Ffrwdgrech Industrial Estate, Brecon, Powys.

Nectar Imports, Quarry Estate, Mere, Wilts BA12 6LA.

Nethergate Brewery Co Ltd, 11–13 High Street, Clare, Suffolk CO10 8NY.

North Cornwall Agencies, Trencreek Farmhouse, Blisland, Bodmin, Cornwall.

Northern Real Ale Agency, Basement Ford 6, Hoults Estate, Walker Road, Newcastle upon Tyne, Tyne & Wear NE6 2HL.

Pilsner Urquell Co Ltd, Fanshaw House, 3–9 Fanshaw Street, London N1 6JU.

Robert Porter & Co Ltd, Unit 2, Pacific Wharf, Hertford Road, Barking, Essex IG11 8BL.

Premium Beer & Wine Co Ltd, Hawks Road, East Gateshead Industrial Estate, Gateshead, Newcastle upon Tyne.

Real Ale Off-licence, 47 Lovat Road, Preston, Lancs.
Ringwood Brewery, 138 Christchurch Road, Ringwood, Hants BH24 3AP.

Samuel Smith Ltd, The Old Brewery, High Street, Tadcaster, N. Yorks LS24 9SB.
San Miguel UK, International House, 174 Three Bridges Road, Crawley, W Sussex RH110 1LE.
Shepherd Neame Ltd, 17 Court Street, Faversham, Kent ME13 7AX.
Small Beer: branches at 91 Newlands St West, Lincoln; 199 Grimsby Road, Cleethorpes, Humberside; 57 Archer Street, Sheffield 8, S Yorks.

Trappist Beer Imports, 95 Westgate Close, Canterbury CT2 8JP, Kent.

Warsteiner UK Ltd, PO Box 40, Essex CB11 4ET.
Charles Wells Ltd, The Brewery, Bedford MK40 4LU.
West Country Products Ltd, 4 Ascot Road, Bedfont, nr Feltham, Mddx TW14 8QH.
M G Winter Imports Ltd, 11 Beaumont Road, London W4 5AG.

York Beer Shop, 28 Sandringham Street, Fishergate, York, N Yorks.

Try also branches of Gateway, Majestic Wines, Oddbins, Safeway, Sainsbury, Tesco and Waitrose.

For more information about German beer imports contact CMA, CMA House, 17a Church Road, Wimbledon, London SW19 5DQ.

INDEX

Italics are used to indicate brewery names.